# GLIMPS INTO SUTTON'S PAST

## Part II
## 1851-1885

**APS BOOKS**
**Stourbridge**

APS Books,
4 Oakleigh Road, Stourbridge, West Midlands, DY8 2JX

APS Books is a subsidiary of the
APS Publications imprint
www.andrewsparke.com

Copyright ©2021 Stephen Roberts
All rights reserved.

Stephen Roberts has asserted his right to be identified as the author of this work in accordance with the Copyright Designs and Patents Act 1988
First published worldwide by APS Books in 2021

No part of this publication may be reproduced, stored in or introduced into a retrieval system, or transmitted, in any form, or by any means (electronic, mechanical, photocopying, recording or otherwise) without the written permission of the publisher except that brief selections may be quoted or copied without permission, provided that full credit is given.

A catalogue record for this book is available from the British Library

**ISBN 978-1-78996-281-9**

IMAGES

Cover image: The Royal Hotel and railway terminus, c. 1865. Reproduced by courtesy of Sutton Coldfield Library.
All other images reproduced by kind permission of Sutton Coldfield Library except for *The Railway Line through Sutton Park*, *Gum Slade, Sutton Park* and *The Woods, Sutton Park* all from the collection of the author.

For Paul Wallis

## Acknowledgements

I wish to record my thanks to Kerry Osbourne who read with great care each chapter of this book as it was written. I am indebted to Yvonne Moore who used her genealogical skills to provide me with a great deal of detail derived from the census returns. To my very great pleasure, I was shown round the town hall built in 1859, and now in the care of the Freemasons, by N.T. Malden, who many years ago taught me at Bishop Vesey's Grammar School. I would like to note the invaluable work Janet Jordan has done in transcribing and making available online the fascinating diary of nineteenth century Sutton resident Sarah Holbeche. My thanks are also due to Len Smith for sharing with me his knowledge of private lunatic asylums. At Sutton Coldfield Library Abigail Collingwood has, as usual, been very efficient and very supportive of my work. The images of Wyndley Pool, Gum Slade and the woods of Sutton Park are taken from the collection of the author. All other images which appear in this book are reproduced by courtesy of Sutton Coldfield Library. A final word of thanks to Andrew Sparke who has supported this ongoing project with enthusiasm.

## CONTENTS

Introduction: A Changing Town  1

I: The Slow Death of The Corporation  13

II: The Arrival Of The Railway  23

III: Crime  34

IV: Schools  41

V: Leisure  52

# INTRODUCTION: A CHANGING TOWN

On 25 January 1858 Victoria, Princess Royal, the eldest daughter of Queen Victoria and Prince Albert, married Prince Frederick William of Prussia at the Chapel Royal, St. James Palace. This event was marked by celebrations across the country. The corporation of Sutton Coldfield, made up of 25 wealthy men, took great pride in their royal charters and arranged for food and drink to be provided for the elderly residents of the ten almshouses and, separately, for the park keepers and foresters they employed and, in the evening, gathered for their own private dinner. Signing himself 'A Suttonian', an inhabitant reflected on the day:

'The entertainment to the inmates of the almshouses and the corporation servants (comprising very few persons) was provided out of corporation funds and not out of the pockets of its members. The dinner was confined to those who could afford to pay. Nothing was provided for the poor; neither was there any general rejoicing as in other places. Several old women went round begging for coppers to enable them to have a tea-drinking … The corporation negatived a proposition by one of its members that the old people should be provided with a dinner by subscription; and contented themselves and a few of the richer inhabitants with a dinner … There are many rooms in the parish where the poor might have assembled, and, through the kindness of their richer neighbours, have had cause to remember with pleasure the Princess' marriage. As it is, they will long call it to mind with rankling hearts as an occasion on which the rich met together, feasted and drank, and the poor went empty away.' [1]

This letter makes clear that, in the third quarter of the nineteenth century, Sutton was not a town at ease with itself. In fact it was a deeply divided town – perhaps more so than at any point in its history. The divisions were between a rich elite of men with deep roots in the town, many of them gentleman farmers, and a rich elite of men, many of them members of the professions or manufacturers, who felt that they were outsiders. The bitter wrangling that these divisions produced over shooting and hunting rights in

---

[1] *Birmingham Daily Post,* 3 February 1858. The ten almshouses were located in Mill Street. By the end of the period covered in this book another four had been erected in both Walmley and Hill and another two in Boldmere.

Sutton Park, over the building of a railway line through the park and over the perpetuation of an unelected corporation is an important theme in this book.

*A view of Sutton c.1870*

The parish of Sutton Coldfield at this time comprised 12,477 acres, including the 2,082 acres of Sutton Park. It was primarily a market town, surrounded by extensive farmland. By 1880 only about 150 acres were built on. By that time there were some 1,564 houses in the parish, 114 built in the previous four years. The town consisted of 'principally one street, on the road from Birmingham to Lichfield, the houses being chiefly of red brick and of handsome appearance.' [2] Along with Francis Bayliss, the butcher, Richard Bromwich, the baker, Edwin Aston, the grocer, and other shopkeepers, Harry Bromwich operated the Post Office in the High Street. Letters were received from Birmingham twice a day and sent to that town twice a day, and pillar boxes could be found in Maney, Wylde Green, Oscott and Hill. The fire station was located in Coleshill Street, as was the police station until it moved to Mill Street. There had been a steady growth in the population of the town – from 4,574 in 1851 to 7,737 in 1881. The largest concentration of population was in Sutton itself, including Maney, with 2,902 inhabitants. In Boldmere there were 1,967 inhabitants, in Hill 1,381 and in Walmley 788.

---

[2] *Directory of Sutton Coldfield 1880.*

The total length of roads amounted to just over 22 miles, including about ten miles of turnpike roads.

*Sutton Fire Brigade c.1885*

The vast majority of the inhabitants of Sutton worked in agriculture – as carpenters, wheelwrights, blacksmiths, coopers, shepherds and, especially, as labourers. We can learn something about their lives from the census returns. For example, we find Joseph Whitelock, John Mullins and Joseph Reynolds living in Maney in 1861. Whitelock, aged 59 and married to Hannah, was a farm labourer, as were his three sons Benjamin, William and Thomas, aged between 11 and 15. Three of his five younger children were at school, as were most children up to ten from farming families. John Mullins, aged 40 and married to Bridget, was also a farm labourer and his two sons aged 19 and 14 did the same work, with two of his other four children at school. There was also a lodger, William Barratt, another labourer, living in the house. It is not uncommon to read in the census returns of farm labourers taking in lodgers to supplement their incomes. For farm labourers the work was arduous, hours were long, wages were poor and they did it for all their lives. Joseph Reynolds, aged 40 and married to Martha, was a little more prosperous. A wheelwright, with four children (two of them at school) and two apprentice wheelwrights sharing the accommodation, he was able to afford a servant.

The wire-drawing mill at Penns operated by Baron Dickinson Webster and his partner James Horsfall provided employment for over one hundred men living in Walmley. [3] The wire drawers were well paid, earning between 40 shillings and 60 shillings a week. In 1851 Joseph Brandon was a wire puller, aged 36 and living with his wife Sarah. Of their five children, the eldest was, at the age of twelve, working as a stable boy. He may have been provided with this job by Brandon's neighbour, a farm bailiff Joseph Davenport. Labourers at the Penns mill earned 18s a week. It was much better pay than working in the fields. When the mill closed in 1859 many of the skilled wire drawers moved to the new site at Hay Mills, but others lost their jobs completely.

The closure of the mill at Penns offered proof, if proof was needed, to the working people of Sutton that employment, and also being able to work, were precarious things. A branch of the North Warwickshire Medical and Friendly Society was established in the town in 1845 to provide small payments and visits by doctors for members too unwell to work. By 1852 this had recruited almost 100 members, as well as a number of gentlemen as honorary subscribers. These honorary members 'only needed to see that the labouring classes could help themselves to put their shoulders to the wheel and give the labourers a lift.' [4] At that point the society had funds of £334. 5s. In 1862 the branch seceded from its parent body to become the Sutton Coldfield Benefit Society, with funds of £218. 18. 8d. To promote their societies the members had an annual meeting each June in which they marched in procession to Holy Trinity carrying their banner reading 'Piety, Prudence and Charity' and accompanied by a brass band, where the rector delivered a sermon. This was followed by a dinner, an afternoon of entertainment in Sutton Park and, finally, supper. The ambition was to

---

[3] See S. Roberts, *Webster & Horsfall & the Atlantic Cable* (Birmingham, 2020), pp. 17-24.
[4] *Aris's Birmingham Gazette,* 7 June 1852.

recruit all labourers who lived in the parish, but only a tiny minority of working men became involved.

*St Michael's Church built 1856-1857*

For the newly-installed rector William Kirkpatrick Riland Bedford the defence of the Anglican religion was at the top of his list of priorities. He was concerned that there was no Anglican church in Boldmere – then known as the Coldfield – and that the inhabitants might fall under the influence of 'the Romanists' who had built a seminary at Oscott. [5] A committee, with Riland Bedford as its chairman and including the solicitors Henry Addenbrooke and Richard Sadler and the physician Thomas Chavasse, was formed in May 1853 with the intention of raising subscriptions and donations to fund the building of a new church.

These efforts included a bazaar held in Sutton Park in June 1854, with the prospect of being served at stalls by Lady Hartopp and other aristocratic

---

[5] Ibid., 25 December 1854.

ladies. That event apart, it proved to be hard going. The committee met on 28 occasions, with members coming and going. By December 1854 £1,600 had been raised, but the projected cost of £3,000 was still a long way from being met. The London architect J.F. Wadmore drew up 'a handsome design suitable to the claims of the Church of England', but, when he arrived in Sutton with his plans, only Riland Bedford was there to meet him. [6] It was only with great difficulty that a builder, Isaac Highway of Walsall, was found – and Riland Bedford needed to guarantee £1,000 for work to begin. Finally, in September 1856, the foundation stone was laid in front of 3-400 people, and one year later St. Michael's Church, built of limestone, was consecrated. By 1859 a new road from Wylde Green to St Michael's was being constructed. Riland Bedford selected the Revd. E. H. Kittoe as the incumbent. He was described by a visitor who attended one of his services as 'a tall gentleman of about five and fifty years, with a greyish beard ... and eyes that scanned the church with somewhat of suspicion.' [7] Kittoe was to play a leading role in the public affairs of Sutton, 'and took great interest in gardening and was a successful grower and exhibitor of roses.' [8] He died in February 1894.

*Interior of St. Michael's Church*

---

[6] Ibid., 22 January 1855.
[7] Quoted in E.M. Joiner, *The Parish Church of St. Michael, Boldmere, 1857-1957* (Sutton Coldfield, 1957).
[8] *Birmingham Daily Post,* 23 February 1894.

Though there were small congregations of Baptists meeting in the High Street and of Primitive Methodists and Wesleyan Methodists meeting in 'the small chapel at Maney – poor almost to the point of shutting down', they did not have permanent ministers and the town lacked a true place of worship for Nonconformists. [9] In 1877 a committee of men from Sutton, Erdington and Birmingham was formed with the intention of rectifying the situation. The cost of building a Congregationalist chapel was calculated at being about £2,000 – it eventually rose to £3,000 – and was to be met by individual donations. These donations did not generally exceed £150. A site was purchased in Park Road, and George Ingall of Birmingham was appointed as architect. He drew up plans for a building to accommodate 636 people, but, in its first stage, the chapel provided seats for 300 people on the floor and 100 in the end gallery. The builders were the Horsley Brothers, who had erected a number of board schools in Aston and Birmingham. A large crowd gathered for the laying of the foundation stone in July 1879, and were addressed by the well-known Congregationalist minister R.W. Dale of Carr's Lane Chapel in Birmingham. This 'commodious and beautiful place of worship' opened April 1880. [10]

The most notable new building erected during these years, however, was in the centre of Sutton, at the foot of Mill Street. This was a new town hall, and it was funded by compensation of £3,000 paid to the corporation by the London & North Western Railway Company after it had failed to build a railway line from Birmingham, which, according to an agreement made in 1846, would include a stop at Sutton. Though claims to spend some of this sum on the new church at Boldmere or on Bishop Vesey's Grammar School were put forward, the trustees of the fund, the warden Baron D. Webster, the rector W.K. Riland Bedford and the physician George Bodington, were united in their belief that it should be used to build a new town hall. They found themselves supported by an inhabitant in a letter pretending to be written by the town hall built by Bishop Vesey and demolished in 1854:

'The glory of your town is departed. The annual festivals are put an end to. That most interesting of your sights – the assemblage of some hundred children, who yearly give full swing to their mirthful enjoyment on Whit Monday – can meet no more. You, yourselves, have no suitable place to

---

[9] *Aris's Birmingham Gazette,* 28 May 1855.
[10] *Birmingham Daily Post,* 6 April 1880. This building is now known as the United Reformed Church.

assemble in ... Who is to blame? Is the old corporation in fault? If not, who then? It cannot be for want of funds because I know you have three thousand pounds which can be made applicable at once; and if that not be sufficient, surely the corporation will find the remainder of the money to erect a noble and suitable edifice to be at once an ornament, a benefit and a convenience to the town?' [11]

There was a delay of several years in acting as disputes arose over the location for the new building. The site of the old town hall in the marketplace at the top of Mill Street was deemed not sufficiently large; plans to erect a statue in that place of Bishop Vesey also came to nothing. It was eventually decided by the corporation that the new town hall should be erected on land it owned at the bottom of Mill Street – though not deemed the best site, it was one that did not require land to be purchased. Watched by 700 pupils from the corporation schools – who also sang the 100$^{th}$ Psalm - and many of the inhabitants, the first stone of the town hall was laid by Anna Maria Webster, the wife of the warden, in August 1858.

Another ceremony in September 1859 marked the opening of the new building designed by the Wolverhampton architect George Bidlake and costing £4,400. 'A handsome luncheon by the corporation, professional singers and new era opened on Sutton Coldfield', Sarah Holbeche noted in her diary.[12] Two storeys high, the town hall consisted, on the ground floor, of a library, a surveyor's office, a magistrates' court and two cells and, on the first floor, of a large corporation room. From the tower there were excellent views of Sutton Park. The town, it was believed, had acquired a town hall 'suitable to its increasing importance.' [13] For twenty years the inhabitants of Sutton used their town hall for public meetings, lectures, theatrical performances and balls. Then, in 1879, concerns arose about the structure. The corporation commissioned William Tait, an architect, to examine the building. He reported that, owing to the poor construction of the roof, the walls were bulging by between four and five inches out of the perpendicular. The corporation decided that dancing could not continue in

---

[11] *Aris's Birmingham Gazette,* 28 May 1855.
[12] sclhrg.org.uk/research/transcriptions/2536-sarah-holbeche-diary.html?start=43, p. 51.
[13] *Aris's Birmingham Gazette.,* 3 September 1859.

the building until repairs had been carried out. The bill for making the town hall safe was considerable.

*The Town Hall on Mill Street*

A few years before the town hall was opened another new structure had appeared close to the centre of Sutton. This was the gasworks in Coleshill Street. Before then oil lamps had lit the main streets. This method of street lighting had disappeared decades earlier in Birmingham, with gas lighting being three times brighter. Plans were drawn up to establish a private company to provide gas lighting in the main streets of Sutton. At a public meeting in February 1853 the Sutton Coldfield Gas Light & Coke Company was launched. [14] The capital needed was £2,500 and this would be raised by an issue of shares at £1 each. It seemed such a promising business venture that many of the shares were snapped up at the meeting. A contract for construction of the new gasworks was agreed with a London gas engineer, Alfred Penny, and, in autumn 1855, the first gas lights were lit in the heart of Sutton. A small number of householders were also able to arrange for a supply of gas.

It turned out, however, that the gasworks were 'quite inadequate' – the works were too small and lacked adequate supplies of coal and, in addition, a limited number of pipes had been laid. [15] In April 1864 an attempt was made by a number of Sutton gentlemen, including George Bodington and Henry Addenbrooke, to re-launch the business. The aim was to raise £4,000 by issuing 400 shares at a price of £10 each. Most of these shares were sold to existing shareholders, with the remainder being made available to new investors. Sarah Holbeche was not impressed by developments. 'Additions to the gasworks and tall chimney intruding itself to sight ... Gas stoves substituted for coal fires in church, not promising as to result.' [16]

During the summer, when little gas was used, the works were able to cope, but 'at those periods of the year when we need gas most then is there little to be had.' [17] In December 1875 the supply failed when the gasworks were flooded. Residents had to resort, as they had twenty years earlier, to oil lamps and candles. The manager of the works, Henry Richards, braced himself for the complaints, but it was the chairman, choosing not to identify himself in the press, who sought to explain the situation: 'The water had settled to such an extent directly under the furnaces and retorts that it became difficult to make gas at all and impossible to make in sufficient quantity to meet the demand by the consumers. ' [18] Two years later the south side of the town

---

[14] sclhrg.org.uk/research/transcriptions/2536-sarah-holbeche-diary.html?start=38, 29 September 1852, p. 41 indicates that before this a tentative start had been made installing a limited gas supply in Sutton: 'Gas opened. A lecture in the town hall by Mr George Bodington and fireworks. The church, a few houses, 4 lights in town hall and police station only lighted this year.'
[15] *Birmingham Daily Post,* 24 April 1865.
[16] sclhrg.org.uk/research/transcriptions/2536-sarah-holbeche-diary.html?start=53, October, 27 November 1864, pp.69, 71.
[17] *Birmingham Daily Post,* 8 December 1875,
[18] Ibid., 13 December 1875.

was supplied with gas by the town council in Birmingham – to the great discomfort of several members of the corporation who saw the intrusion of their neighbour as 'most arbitrary and tyrannical.' [19] However, the writing was on the wall for the Sutton Coldfield Gas Light & Coke Company.

There was concern in the town about the increasing involvement in its affairs of Birmingham. Indeed some inhabitants spoke openly of the intention of Birmingham to take over its smaller neighbour; and in her diary Sarah Holbeche expressed her dismay at the installation of the retired Birmingham solicitor as warden: 'Mr Colmore – re-elected a regular? Brumagem party – Sutton represented by Brum.' [20] These fears manifested themselves in resistance to a plan in 1864-5 by the Birmingham Waterworks Company to sink a shaft in Sutton Park and draw water from its streams. Birmingham was already provided with forty million gallons of water a week by the company from the river Tame and brooks in Aston and Witton, but its population was steadily growing and Sutton Park offered an excellent source of pure water. The waterworks company sought an act of parliament to extend its activities beyond Birmingham. 'Plans out for water works neither with our leave or by it; such is the presumption of Birmingham!', Sarah Holbeche indignantly observed. [21] Local opinion ranged from constraining the 'simply enormous' powers being sought by the company to outright opposition on the grounds that they would 'turn the park into an arid desert – like the deserts of Africa.' [22] 'Let the Birmingham Waterworks Company once get into the park', one alarmed opponent declared, 'and they would do as they liked until the parish would be turned into a vast reservoir for the supply of Birmingham.' [23] At the committee stage of the bill in the House of Lords in May 1865, a barrister employed by the corporation argued that the plans would do great injury to the park. The committee was persuaded that this would be the case, and the clause to draw water from Sutton Park was struck out of the bill. 'Water works victory – not quite managed by Brum! "Thank God for a House of Lords"', Sarah Holbeche wrote triumphantly in

---

[19] *Birmingham Daily Gazette,* 9 October 1877.
[20] schlhrg.org.uk/research/transcriptions/2536-sarah-holbeche-diary.html?start=63, 2 November 1865, p. 83
[21] sclhrg.org.uk/research/transcriptions/2536-sarah-holbeche-diary.html?start=54, 5 December 1864, p. 71
[22] *Birmingham Journal,* 17 December 1864.
[23] Ibid.

her diary. [24] It was not a victory to be repeated seven years later when plans were drawn up to build a railway line across Sutton Park.

An indication that the influence of Birmingham on Sutton was growing came with the closure of the local bank. Established in 1819, the Sutton Coldfield Savings Bank was situated in the town hall and opened on the first Monday of each month. The manager was paid an annual salary of £711 19s, and had an unpaid assistant. At the beginning of 1862, the bank had 441 depositors with savings amounting to £12,890. It was a small bank and there were often rumours in the town that it was closing, but these were always firmly denied. In January 1870, however, it was announced that the bank would cease activity. Suttonians were asked to attend the bank over four days in February to withdraw their savings or transfer them to another bank. The destination of most of this money was Lloyds Bank, established in Birmingham in 1765 and operating on the High Street in Sutton since 1864.

---

[24] schlhrg.org.uk/research/transcriptions/2536-sarah-holbeche-diary.html?start=60, July 1865, p. 79.

# I: THE SLOW DEATH OF THE CORPORATION

When the ratepayers of the neighbouring town of Birmingham elected their first councillors in December 1838, the warden and society in Sutton Coldfield felt nothing but relief that they had escaped the process. The Municipal Corporations Act 1835 had replaced 178 closed corporations with elected town councils, but a number of places had been excluded. Amongst these were Sittingbourne in Kent, Henley-on-Thames in Oxfordshire, Alnwick in Northumberland - and Sutton Coldfield. The warden and society in Sutton Coldfield had been in existence since 1528, and consisted of 25 men, drawn almost exclusively from the wealthy elite. A number of members served on the corporation for decades. The physician George Bodington, who owned a private lunatic asylum and a sanatorium for tuberculosis patients in Maney, was a member for almost thirty three years. His regular contributions to meetings were invariably in defence of the status quo and he was one of the last to accept reform. And then there was Thomas Wilkins, who, after his family had sent in his resignation without telling him, declared that he 'meant to die as one of Sutton corporation.' [25]

When one of the members of the corporation resigned or died, he was replaced by another gentleman. Occasionally two gentlemen might be nominated and then a vote amongst the members of the corporation to decide who to admit would take place; it was the closest the corporation came to any form of democracy. When one member of the corporation J.G. Todd declared that elections to a town council would be 'a disturbance ... (which) would greatly annoy a large number of the inhabitants', he was expressing a view shared by many of his colleagues. [26] Over time a number of members of the corporation – such as the physician James Johnstone - became supporters of reform, but it was not until 1886 that an elected town council came into existence. The warden and society offered resistance and obstruction and then fell back on procrastination and delay.

During the years covered by this book eleven men occupied the post of warden. They were elected each November, always without contest. The

---

[25] *Birmingham Daily Post,* 13 February 1877.
[26] Ibid., 30 May 1879.

appointment was then followed by a sumptuous dinner paid for from corporation funds, which was controversial in the town and eventually became a standing joke, the symbol of all that was wrong with a closed corporation. There were occasions when it proved difficult to find a member of the corporation to accept the role of warden, but it has to be said that many of the men who did come forward had ability and a desire to do what, on their terms, was best for the town. Four of the wardens were physicians: George Bodington (1852-3), Thomas Chavasse (1862-3), James Johnstone (1876-8) and Henry Duncalfe (1882-5); three were clergymen: William Kirkpatrick Riland Bedford (1854-5), Edward Kittoe (1867-70) and Montagu Webster (1874-5); and one was a solicitor Thomas Eddowes (1871-3).

*Gum Slade, Sutton Park*

The income of the corporation was derived primarily from rents and investments and then from the sale of timber from felled trees, visitors' tickets and fines from Sutton Park. This money was spent on such requirements for the corporation schools as repairs and books, maintaining the alms houses, blankets for the poor, the fire engine and the salaries of the deputy steward – a solicitor who acted as town clerk - the schoolteachers, the park keepers, the inspector of weights and measures and labourers. The park committee was particularly attentive in overseeing the felling of trees, and would themselves periodically inspect those identified for removal and take into account the effect on the picturesqueness of the park. Regulations were issued to control activities in the park – in spring 1853 permission for a steeplechase was refused and parties admitted only on four days of the week and that summer, with game 'almost annihilated', the shooting of birds and the shooting or coursing of hares and rabbits was prohibited for both inhabitants and non-inhabitants, and walking and riding was confined to the paths and ridings.[27]

The regulations issued by the corporation forcefully reminded the local population that it was an unelected body 'with perpetual power to elect their successors to office.' [28] This sense of injustice seems to have been felt particularly strongly by those who had left Birmingham and made their homes in Sutton. In the early months of 1854 the Sutton Park Protection Society – subsequently known as the Sutton Coldfield Protection Society - emerged to campaign for a new charter of incorporation. With the silversmith Henry Fielding as chairman and the accountant and auctioneer George St. Clair as secretary, it was supported by 'many persons of influence in the neighbourhood' such as the farmer John Buggins and the maltster Joseph Fulford, and clearly well-funded, able to distribute handbills to all residents of Sutton calling on them to sign a petition to be presented to the warden George Bodington to authorize a public meeting at the town hall. [29] Well-attended meetings were held at the Old Sun in March and April, where it was heard that the warden had refused permission for a public meeting and privately advised Fielding 'to be cautious ... there are those about him who have an interest in misleading him.' [30] Fielding replied by declaring that 'they knew more than some members of that body would like to hear of.' [31]

The public meeting went ahead anyway, when privately-owned land at Clifton Hill was made available to the demonstrators. It was described as a 'wonderful' event, attended by up to 1,500 people and reminded St. Clair of the famous meeting on Newhall Hill in Birmingham during the

---

[27] *Aris's Birmingham Gazette,* 19 September 1853. Also see ibid., 21 August for regulations for that season, setting out the days and hours when shooting and coursing could take place and the number of dogs and beaters that could be present.

[28] *Birmingham Journal,* 4 March 1854.

[29] Ibid., 1 April 1854.

[30] Ibid.

[31] Ibid.

parliamentary reform agitation of 1832. [32] The speeches lasted for three hours. Fielding, who had experience of political meetings in Birmingham, offered a sober assessment of the situation:

'The world was against close corporations. There wasn't a thoughtful man in England who did not abhor the principle of irresponsible self-selection and, by assembling that day in such numbers, the men of Sutton were showing that they were determined to carry out amongst themselves the true principles of representative government. The present corporation had worn their original dress more than 300 years and rather queer they nowadays looked in it.'

It was left to St. Clair to inject humour into the proceedings:

'The charter ... gave the inhabitants the power to hunt or fish in the park; but who had the use of the fish pools now? My Lord Tomnoddy claimed one and Peter McGooselem claimed a second and Harry Snooks claimed a third; and there were keepers in the park who, if they found anyone except the aforementioned McGooselem, Snooks and co. throwing a line in the pools, would seize the offender by the neck and drag him off to prison ... As for hunting, the only game left them was the corporation and, now that the dogs had been loosed at its heels, he hoped some excellent sport was before the inhabitants that they would follow up to the death and take good care was never dug out again.'[33]

So the petition to Queen Victoria was launched and collecting signatures and organising meetings kept up the momentum. At the Emmanuel College Arms in May, it was reported to a 'numerous' attendance that a deputation had met George Frederick Muntz and William Scholefield, the two MPs for Birmingham, and Charles Geach, MP for Coventry, for three hours at the Reform Club in London before being cordially received by the Home Secretary Palmerston, who promised to send a commissioner to investigate the situation. [34] Whilst they waited for this to happen, the Sutton Park Protection Society continued to hold meetings to assert that the unelected corporation had no legal right to regulate 'sporting' in the park. One leading

---

[32] Ibid., 15 April 1854.
[33] Ibid.
[34] Ibid., 27 May 1854.

member of the campaign Edward Lewis decided to test this proposal – and, as a result, faced legal action from the corporation. Meanwhile, a fete in the park in July, offering dancing, cricket, boating and a band, topped up the funds of the campaign.

It was not until August 1855 that the commission of inquiry, led by Major George Warburton, arrived in Sutton to gather evidence for the Privy Council.[35] Both the local campaign and the corporation were represented by barristers. It was argued that the corporation had not managed the park effectively, felling healthy oaks, failing to plant chestnut, larch and birch trees which were suitable for the soil and not undertaking dressing and cropping, which had led to an income much lower than could be expected. In response it was stated that the park had been well-managed, with members of the corporation joining their surveyor Charles Cooper to inspect what was being done and the rights of pasturing cattle and removing gorse, ling, brown peas, sand and gravel in carts being of great value to the inhabitants. In addition the corporation's barristers drew attention to the fact that attendance at the monthly meetings was 'generally pretty numerous', that the schools were well regarded by local clergymen and that blankets and baby linen had been provided for inhabitants who were Catholics.[36] They also challenged signatures on the petition, some of which were struck off. Warburton took away with him 400 pages of notes. The Privy Council considered the evidence, and its report was published at the end of the year. The petition for reform was rejected, though the corporation was instructed to conduct an independent audit and to publish their accounts. 'The low party defeated. Corporation came off in flying colours …', Sarah Holbeche noted in her diary, reflecting the feelings of the Sutton establishment.[37] With this defeat and 'after much labour and considerable expense', the Protection Society was wound up.[38]

---

[35] Major George Warburton served in the Royal Artillery from 1833 until 1854, when he retired on full pay. He was elected Liberal MP for Harwich in 1857, but, whilst suffering from indigestion, shot himself through the head later that year.

[36] *Aris's Birmingham Gazette,* 22 August 1855.

[37] sclhrg.org.uk/research/transcriptions/2536-sarah-holbeche-diary.html?start=40, p. 45.

[38] *Aris's Birmingham Gazette*, 5 January 1855.

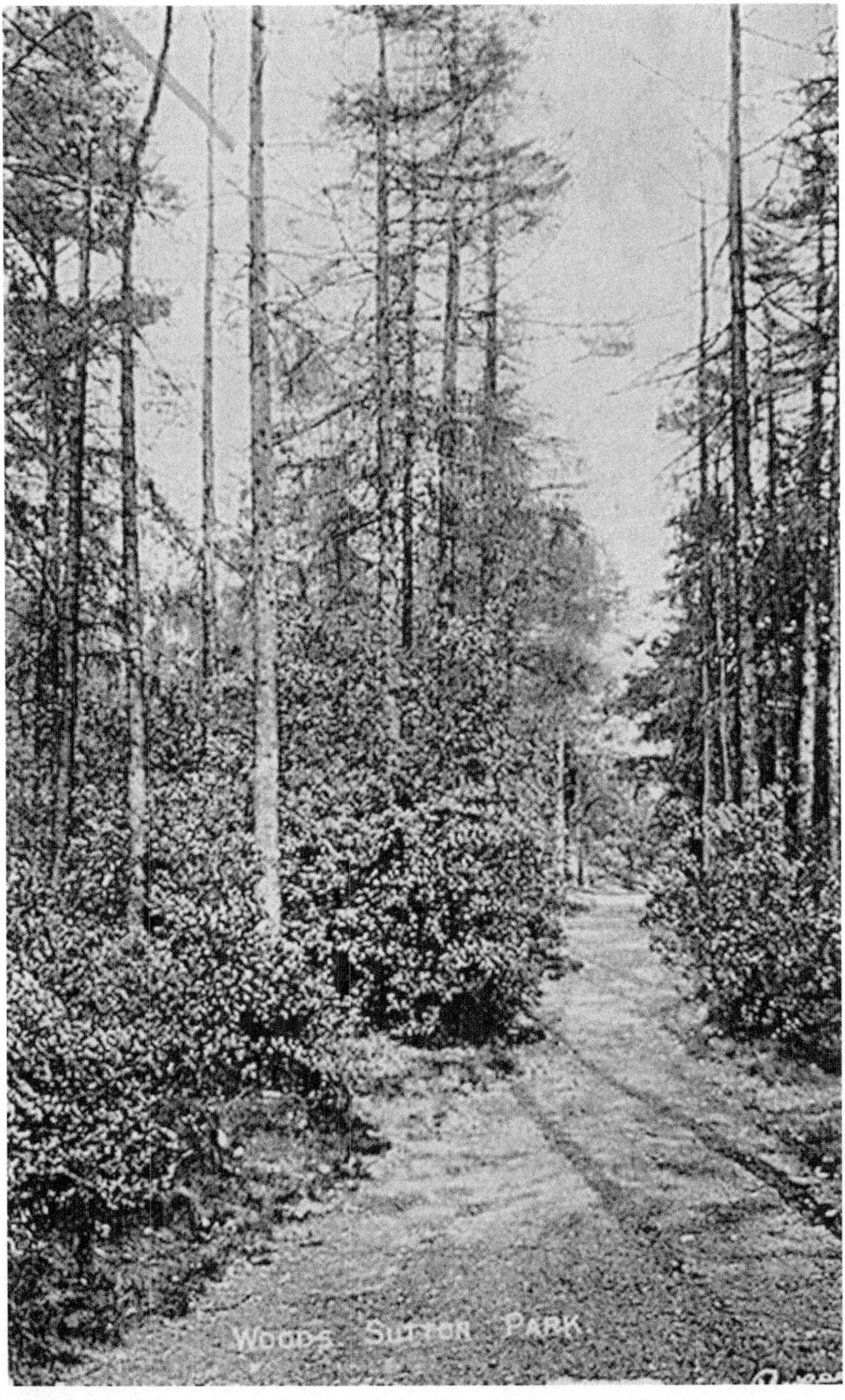
WOODS SUTTON PARK

Inevitably there were recriminations. The reformers believed that they had been betrayed by the Penns wire manufacturer Baron D. Webster, a member of the corporation who professed Liberal opinions:

'With Baron Webster's fine professions, we might expect him to have given us his help and assistance; but, when the hour of need came, he not only refused to sign our petition but used his influence to defeat our plans. At the enquiry before the commissioner, he came forward as a witness and said that sporting in Sutton Park was the divine right of members of the corporation alone; and that park could not be improved for the benefit of the inhabitants; indeed everything that he could do to prevent us having local self-government he did and continues to do …' [39]

The corporation now entered a period of public calm, but its critics were not entirely silenced. The warden's dinner held each November and paid for from corporation funds was an obvious target. In 1859 120 men sat down to their 'magnificent repast', sixty of them guests. [40] A defence of the event labelled those who complained as 'ignorant and misguided' and enquired, 'Have they (the corporation) not the perfect right … to decide as to the application of the trust funds without asking the opinion of the inhabitants, most of whom are not fitted by position or education to have a voice in the matter?' [41] Sincerely-held as they might have been, these remarks, in 1859, were undoubtedly unwise.

In 1870 a new campaign for reform of the corporation was launched. The Association for the Protection of the Rights of the Inhabitants came into existence and claimed that the coporation was denying gentlemen their right to shoot in the park and the much-vaunted corporation schools 'were merely making agricultural labourers of the children.' [42] Its secretary John Hibell, a retired manager of a wire manufactory, sent a printed letter to the warden the Revd. E.H. Kittoe and the members of the corporation arguing that, when vacancies arose, they should be filled by nominations from the inhabitants. At a public meeting that September Edward Arthurs, a rate collector, James Fawdry, a corn dealer, and James Motteram, a barrister who lived at Maney

---

[39] Quoted in S. Roberts *Webster & Horsfall & the Atlantic Cable* (Birmingham, 2019), pp. 4-5.
[40] *Birmingham Daily Post,* 2 January 1871.
[41] Ibid., 5 October 1859.
[42] *Birmingham Daily Gazette,* 10 November 1869.

House, were put forward. J.C. Cull, a schoolmaster and churchwarden from Holy Trinity, was there to speak for the corporation. Arthurs, however, who had not been present at the meeting, immediately disassociated himself from the campaign. With that, the campaign spluttered to an end. It had proved to be 'of a very uninfluential character.' [43]

Yet it was clear that reform of the corporation could not be put off indefinitely. The warden and society did not have the will or the powers to implement the important requirements now expected of local government. The difficulties crystallized around the issue of public health. Sutton was supplied with water from wells (such as that in Mill Street) and pumps (such as that in Coleshill Street). Sewage was absorbed into gardens or flowed into ditches and then into Plants Brook. The roads were watered by the highway board, which was paid for by subscriptions from householders, supplemented, from the 1870s, by an annual contribution of £20 from the corporation. What all this led to was that Sutton had a higher death rate (17.8 per 1,000) than Saltley (13 per 1,000).

At the end of 1870 the corporation received a deputation, mandated by a public meeting, made up of weighty local figures, notably W.K. Riland Bedford, the rector, Albert Smith, the headmaster of the grammar school, and J.T. Chance, the Smethwick glass manufacturer who had become the tenant of Four Oaks Hall. Riland Bedford had resigned as a member of the corporation the previous year in order to lead the campaign for it to re-invent itself as a municipal authority and take responsibility for sewerage and drainage. 'We are not at law with the corporation and you ought not to be at law with us', Motteram observed. 'It is that unfortunate spirit of antagonism which exists and which manifests itself on almost every occasion that is do deeply to be deplored.' [44] It was a cordial meeting and it was agreed to present both sides of the argument to the Attorney General, Sir Robert Collier. The outcome was a decision that the corporation could be seen as a municipal body and able to make use of existing legislation, the Nuisances Removal and Diseases Prevention Act 1860. However, this was then negated, on a question of terminology, by the Public Health Act 1872. The Local Government Board decided that the responsibility for a system of

---

[43] W.K. Riland Bedford, *History of Sutton Coldfield* (Birmingham, 1891), p. 62.
[44] *Birmingham Daily Post*, 2 January 1871.

sewerage in Sutton lay with the Aston Board of Guardians, which began to levy a rate.

For the reformers the corporation was now in its death spiral. In October 1873 Riland Bedford, Motteram, W.R. Wills, a solicitor, and Allen Lepard Crockford, a draper, put their names to a statement that argued that, on the grounds of uncertainty about its powers and its consequent inaction, the corporation needed to be replaced by an elected body. The corporation claimed that some of the allegations in the statement were 'uncalled for' and that it could do nothing without the approval of the inhabitants. [45] Yet most of its members knew that the existing arrangements could not be maintained for much longer. The solicitor T. S. Eddowes, who served as warden at this time, expressed his hope that if 'the lesson that they were destined to learn … could be communicated to them without external aid so much the better.' [46] Yet still there were adjournments and delay. The physician James Johnstone presented himself as the leading reformer on the corporation. In November 1875 he expressed his 'reverence' for the corporation whilst simultaneously putting before it a motion in favour of an elected body. [47] The following month there was a public meeting where the Revd. Montagu Webster, now warden, declared that he would agree with whatever was decided that night, 'whether it pleased him or not.' [48]

A Royal Commission to enquire into, and report on, the unreformed corporations was appointed in April 1876. Whilst this gathered evidence, the corporation in Sutton began to consider some of the more obvious abuses. In July the warden's dinner was discussed, the cost of which had risen to £60. Describing the dinner as 'a monstrous piece of useless extravagance', Albert Smith called for corporation funds to be withdrawn. [49] Bodington, however, dissented and the discussion was adjourned. The issue of self-election was, of course, at the heart of the matter. And so another petition was printed and another public meeting called. 'They are tired of electing one and another', Eddowes observed, 'and he believed the inhabitants were tired in seeing them do it.' [50] Though his doubts about self-

---

[45] Ibid., 10 February 1874.
[46] Ibid., 5 November 1872.
[47] Ibid., 16 November 1875.
[48] Ibid., 18 December 1875.
[49] Ibid., 11 July 1876.
[50] Ibid., 21 March 1876.

election were growing, Bodington declared that they had always elected men who were fit to be members of the corporation.

Having met the warden and four members of the corporation in London, the Hon. T.H.W. Pelham arrived in Sutton in March 1879 to conduct an inquiry into the governance of town on behalf of the Royal Commission. He was presented with two petitions for reform signed by 353 residents and a counter-petition, in which the number of signatories was not revealed. Members of the corporation who supported the establishment of an elected municipal authority – such as the farmers William Walters and Thomas Hayward - and those who did not – such as the Revd. E.W. Robinson and E.W. Simkin - came forward one after another to state their cases and to be cross-examined. The issue of responsibility for the disposal of sewage came up again and again. A proposal that only part of the parish be incorporated made little headway. In truth the corporation had 'had its doom sealed and in a couple of years would be extinct.' [51] Under the Municipal Corporations Act 1883, Sutton was able to present a petition from householders which secured a new charter of incorporation. In the meantime the old corporation continued with its work – awarding £20 each to four poor young women about to be married in April 1883 and, as late as December 1885, electing new members. It declined, however, to join other closed corporations in an attempt to resist the new legislation. When the town council was finally elected in 1886, they were nearly all new men.

---

[51] Ibid., 28 September 1883.

# II: THE ARRIVAL OF THE RAILWAY

Between 1837 and 1842 Birmingham was connected by railway with Liverpool, London, Derby and Gloucester, and there were plans for lines to other places including Dudley, Stourbridge Leicester and Shrewsbury. Inevitably the leading men of Sutton watched all of this with interest. The benefits a railway link with Birmingham might bring became a favoured topic of discussion for the wire manufacturer Baron D. Webster, the farmer John Buggins, the builder Solomon Smith, the physician Joseph Oates, the solicitor Richard Sadler, the headmaster of the grammar school James Eccleston and the proprietor of the Three Tuns Harry Smith. The auctioneer Samuel Kempson went one step further and became a shareholder in two projected railway companies, neither of which were in the event successful.[52]

## *The Birmingham To Sutton Railway*

In April 1846 the Birmingham, Lichfield and Manchester Railway Company signed an agreement with the corporation to build a stop at Sutton. Within months this company was taken over. The London & North Western Railway Company now became responsible for constructing the line between Birmingham and Lichfield. Years passed, however, and it did not get built. A period of wrangling between the corporation and the LNWR over compensation now began. Baron D. Webster represented the corporation in these negotiations and recalled a discussion with the company's solicitor Edward Carter: 'Mr Carter said, "What do you want? We will give you a £10 note for your bond." Mr Carter said that to me.'[53] Eventually compensation of £3,000 was agreed upon.

It was to be several years before the building of a railway line again came to dominate public life in Sutton. There was agreement at several public meetings in the mid-1850s that Sutton was 'in urgent need of railway accommodation'.[54] Coal would be brought cheaply into the town from 'the

---

[52] The Birmingham, West Bromwich, Wednesbury and Walsall Railway Company and the Birmingham and Boston Railway Company.
[53] Quoted in R. Lea *Steaming up to Sutton* (Sutton Coldfield, 1984), p. 11.
[54] *Aris's Birmingham Gazette,* 20 September 1858.

new and almost inexhaustible coalfield of Cannock'. [55] There would also be a reduction in the costs of bringing in Bath stone, which was widely used for building in the town. The timber merchant Thomas Howard was eager to point out that he would have to invest less in supplying timber for the construction of railways. Additionally, the shopkeepers and publicans of the town would also benefit from the increased numbers of visitors to the park. It was not until autumn 1858, however, when the economic climate seemed more propitious, that any plans for a railway line between Birmingham and Sutton Coldfield were actually put forward. There were two rival schemes – an eastern line with the support of the Midland Railway and a western line with the support of the LNWR. Both plans envisaged raising £60,000 through a sale of shares at £10 each. The eastern line was strongly supported by Baron D. Webster, who was much pleased by its close proximity to his mill at Penns. In support of the plan he enlisted George Bodington, Josiah Mason, the pen manufacturer who lived in Erdington, Joseph Dutton who farmed in Sutton, and the physician Thomas Chavasse. These men expected that the proposed railway would be 'a good paying line', with dividends possibly as high as 11%. [56] The western line had the influential support of the rector Riland Bedford and was backed by more of the town's leading figures, notably John Buggins, Henry Fielding, T.S. Eddowes and Samuel Kempson. Its backers declared that, running parallel to the turnpike road, it would be less expensive – the cost not exceeding £9,000 per mile - and a shorter route than its rival. Additionally, with LNWR support, the engines would be able to run into the new station at New Street.

The corporation owned land over which the line would be built and did not need to be persuaded to support the idea. In September 1858 it received deputations from both sides. After questioning supporters and their surveyors, members retired for a 'strongly contested' discussion. [57] After an hour the corporation decided by eleven votes to six to support the western line. Webster, who was at this time warden, did not vote; but he had no intention of giving up on a project that he believed would be so beneficial to his works. After two attempts to arrange some sort of merger with the promoters of the western line came to nothing, Webster was soon vigorously

---

[55] *Birmingham Daily Post,* 28 September 1858.
[56] Ibid., 14 September 1858. Webster had initially supported a western line but managed to extricate himself from this commitment.
[57] Ibid., 21 September 1858.

promoting the scheme he favoured in the newspapers. It was claimed that the cost of the western line would run to £100,000 whereas it could be said 'with unabated confidence' that of the eastern line would not exceed £60,000, making it 'clearly the one which a prudent capitalist would select for the investment of his money.' [58] Unfortunately for Webster and his colleagues, the uptake of shares was not encouraging.

A committee of the House of Commons met over several days in July 1859 to hear the arguments and make a decision. The promoters and their engineers on both sides were called to give evidence. The arguments in favour of the eastern line rested on cost and its effect on the views. James Burke, the engineer employed by the eastern line, pointed out that the rival scheme required more roads to be crossed and also more land (55 acres to 42), the latter meaning that more compensation would need to be paid. He put the cost of the western line at £87,453. Webster's main argument was that the western line 'would enter Sutton at an elevation of nearly fifty feet and would destroy one of the finest views in the kingdom.' [59] Joseph Oates, the physician and former warden who had by now moved to Erdington, claimed that the western line 'would necessitate a very considerable embankment which would destroy the view of the park from the town of Sutton Coldfield.' [60] He added that the inhabitants of Sutton were 'about equally divided … but he thought the more respectable portion were in favour of the eastern route.' [61] These arguments counted for little for 'at the eleventh hour' the western line had been taken over by the LNWR. [62] With its considerable financial resources, the LNWR would, the committee decided, be the builders of the new railway line linking Sutton with the junction at Aston and thus with Birmingham.

The LNWR brought in Eckesley & Read to build the new line. Based in Manchester, William Eckesley's firm did a great deal of work for the LNWR. [63] They, in turn, brought in sub-contractors and, during the nineteen months of construction, 700,000 cubic yards of soil were excavated and

---

[58] Ibid., 3 January 1859.
[59] Ibid., 5 July 1859.
[60] Ibid.
[61] Ibid.
[62] Ibid.
[63] See, for example, *Liverpool Mail,* 7 September 1861 for work the firm undertook on the Birkenhead to Manchester line.

23,000 cubic yards of bricks and timber laid. Bridges had to be built over the Tame and a canal near Gravelly Hill, but beyond Chester Road 'the engineering difficulties ... (were) of a very trifling character.' [64] The work was undertaken by some sixty labourers and was supervised by the engineer of the LNWR Edward Angell and the engineer of Eckesley & Read Mr Acaster, with a foreman, Mr Tait, on the spot each day. In total there were five stops on the line, culminating in Sutton station, built by Charles Burkett of Wolverhampton and described as 'a neat and commodious building in the Italian style.' [65] At one point there was a legal challenge concerning land owned by the Birmingham Waterworks Company, but this was dealt with. The LNWR had indicated that it was prepared to accept some expenditure beyond the estimated cost of £60,000, but this did not prove necessary. [66]

The new railway line received the approval of the Board of Trade and opened a few days later on 2 June 1862, with the first arrival at Sutton being greeted by the warden Josiah Wright, who was headmaster of the grammar school, and several leading townsmen. The journey from Birmingham by omnibus was cut by three quarters of an hour and the cost by half. It was reported that in the afternoon Sutton 'looked quite animated, the visitors who had come by train flowing up the generally quiet streets in continuous streams in the direction of the park ...' [67] One train was made up of 'no fewer than fifteen carriages, all of which were crowded with holiday people ... ' [68] It was estimated that about 2,000 people travelled to Sutton by train on that first day. Meanwhile, the promoters of the railway were enjoying a dinner, with speeches, in the town hall. In his speech the corporation reformer Henry Fielding expressed his pleasure at the building of the new line. Now an LNWR shareholder, he declared that 'the corporation was at last going ahead and he would say that when the corporation was thrown open he would gladly be one of them but he would not be a self-elected man.' [69]

---

[64] *Aris's Birmingham Gazette,* 31 May 1862.
[65] Ibid.
[66] For a detailed description of the route taken by the line and its construction see R. Lea, *Steaming up to Sutton,* pp. 20-39.
[67] *Birmingham Daily Post,* 3 June 1862.
[68] *Aris's Birmingham Gazette,* 3 June 1862.
[69] Ibid.

The timetable for the new line was printed in the local newspapers. [70] The LNWR ran ten engines a day from Sutton to Birmingham, the first leaving at 8.15 am and the last leaving at 8.30 pm. The journey took 35 minutes, with a first class fare costing 1s 6d and a second class 1s 3d. When an engine arrived at Sutton from Birmingham, it was detached from its carriages, moved on to a turntable and rotated so that, with new carriages attached, it could begin its return journey fifteen minutes later. A few days after the opening of the line Sarah Holbeche witnessed 'the sight at night when flocking to return – such as never before had been or could have been seen in this our hitherto quiet locality.' [71]

Suttonians were soon lobbying for the number of trains to be increased. A public meeting in December 1865 appointed a deputation to communicate with the LNWR, which agreed to put on an early train that could meet the train that left New Street for London at 7.30 am and to improve provision on Sunday mornings when some local people attended places of worship in Birmingham. Five years later the LNWR agreed to provide nine more trains, the first one departing at 6.50 am and the last one departing at 11.05 pm. The large numbers using the new railway inevitably led to accidents. The first fatality at Sutton station occurred in February 1866. One Whit Monday 1880 more people were assembled on the platform for the 11.30 pm train to Birmingham than the carriages could hold and James Pepper, a visitor from Liverpool, pushing through the crowd, fell between the footboard and the platform, dying from his injuries a few days later.

Within weeks of the railway opening there was alarm at excursionists 'who have cut down, rooted up and broken the timber trees and underwood, thrown down the gates and fences and done other wilful mischief.' [72] The corporation responded by making clear that anyone apprehended by the park keepers for such behaviour would be prosecuted and banned from entry, with closure of the park an option if the situation did not improve. George Bodington worried that 'Birmingham people would come ... there to build tall chimneys ...' but the manufacturers were far more interested in coming

---

[70] Ibid., 31 May 1862.
[71] sclhrg.org.uk/research/transcriptions/2536-sarah-holbeche-diary.html?=48, 8 June 1862, p. 58
[72] *Birmingham Daily Gazette,* 23 June 1872.

to live in Sutton. [73] There was a great increase in land prices and many houses were built. In the decade after the railway opened the population of Sutton increased from 4,662 to 5,968.

## The Sutton Park Railway

In 1865 approval was given to build a railway line between Wolverhampton and Walsall. This was important to the inhabitants of Sutton Coldfield because the line would run through part of Sutton Park. However, progress was stalled 'on account of some monetary pressure.' [74] The threat to the park was revived in December 1871 when three new proposals were put forward. Two of the possible lines would run along the outskirts of the park, but the third would be built directly through it. [75] Though the corporation decided in January 1872 to object to all three proposals, this was in effect a delaying tactic whilst a decision was made as to which line to support. It was soon clear that it was the Wolverhampton, Walsall and Midland Junction Railway proposal, which would have the greatest impact on the park, that would be at the forefront of public discussion in Sutton. The issue of the new railway was complicated by the fact that a number of members of the corporation, including the warden T.S. Eddowes, were professionally and even financially involved.

Though silent on the matter in public, a major promotor of a railway affecting the park – initially one of the least damaging schemes - was the wire manufacturer James Horsfall. [76] He had bought Penns Hall in 1864 and, at a cost of £70,000, had subsequently built up a substantial stake in the estates of Walmley. Houses were being built on this land, and a railway station in the immediate vicinity would make them more attractive to purchasers. When a public meeting in opposition to the building of a line was called off in March 1862 after a large number of working men sought entry, it was alleged that 'this body of hired roughs' were Horsfall's

---

[73] *Aris's Birmingham Gazette,* 3 June 1872.
[74] *Birmingham Daily Post,* 24 June 1872.
[75] See W.K. Riland Bedford *History of Sutton Coldfield* (Birmingham, 1890), pp. 63-4. David Bramham has written a detailed and considered account of this episode: see schlhrg.org.uk/research/proceedings/146-volume-3/2285-volume-3-article-4-the-railway-line-through-sutton-park.html
[76] The scheme referred to here was known locally as 'Milward's line', on account of the fact that Horsfall used the Birmingham solicitor R.H. Milward to promote it.

employees and had been paid to attend. [77] One of the gentlemen attending the meeting claimed that he had heard it said that "Gaffer has plenty of money and can spare us again any day we are wanted".' [78] Another of those present asked, 'Who paid the railway fare? Who supplied the drink to the invaders? Of course, not those ... who have land to sell or to be improved by the proposed line.' [79] Through his solicitors Horsfall denied being behind the planned disruption; if his employees had been present, they 'did so at their own expense and of their own opinion.' [80] It was an admission, of course, that Horsfall's men were in attendance, though denying that it was at his instigation.

*The railway line through Sutton Park*

There was strenuous opposition to the building of a railway line through the park from a number of leading figures in the town, led by the rector W.K. Riland Bedford. Public discourse in Sutton was to become as bitter as at any time in the nineteenth century. This discourse was carried on through – on occasion ill-tempered - discussions at meetings of the corporation, at public

---

[77] *Birmingham Daily Post,* 9 April 1872.
[78] Ibid., 1 April 1872.
[79] Ibid.
[80] Ibid., 3 April 1872; see ibid., 5 April 1872, for a reply from one of Horsfall's workmen who signs himself 'One of the so-called "roughs"'.

meetings, by the signing of petitions and in the correspondence columns of the newspapers. At corporation meetings Bodington emerged as a forceful advocate of a railway line through the park. His support for the proposal seems to have emerged from his annoyance at the shortage of coal in the town during a recent strike by miners in the Cannock coalfield: a wharf in the park, he believed, would guarantee an alternative supply of coal. His main line of argument over the next few months was to rest on his claim that, as a doughty defender of the park, he was correct when he said that any damage would be minimal. When a petition was presented to the committee of the House of Commons that was considering the railway bill, Bodington dismissed it with contempt. 'The petition was signed by about a dozen men of property and influence in the parish, but the majority of the signatories were those of persons who did not understand the subject, many of them were the signatures of ladies.' [81] Bodington was adamant that the corporation should not launch legal action against the bill – estimating that such a challenge would cost £1-2,000, he declared that the corporation could not afford to so.

For James Johnstone, ensuring that Sutton had a supply of coal did not figure in the motives of the railway's promoters and, making use of an argument he was return to, he argued that, as a physician, he knew the health benefits of the park, which he described as 'one of the lungs of the midland counties.' [82] Sampson Lloyd, who manufactured wheels and axles for steam engines and who had joined the corporation after becoming the tenant of Moor Hall in 1870, offered the damning criticism that the promoters of the railway were 'a set of public adventurers.' [83] The most outspoken critic of the railway scheme amongst corporation members was 'an energetic clergyman called Kittoe.' [84] Declaring that he 'had not one iota of interest in the companies … he had not a shilling invested', the Revd. E.H. Kittoe of St. Michael's, Boldmere, made it clear that he was 'so strongly opposed to the line going through the park that he should leave no stone unturned to defeat it.' [85] This, it turned out, including the making the observation that the judgement of the

---

[81] Ibid., 9 May 1872.
[82] Ibid., 20 February 1872.
[83] Ibid., 1 April 1872.
[84] Ibid., 26 June 1872.
[85] Ibid., 1 April, 22 May 1872.

warden and deputy steward had been 'warped by their prejudices.' [86] Kittoe was in no doubt that the main beneficiaries of the line would be the coal and iron masters. Johnstone and Kittoe were to walk out of a corporation meeting in May 1872.

Both sides of the argument claimed to have won over the majority of the local population, and the purpose of public meetings was to demonstrate the scale of support they had conscripted. The planned meeting of the railway's opponents was abandoned, but its organisers made sure that it was known that large numbers of supporters had turned up. A few days later, in early April, Bodington chaired a meeting of working men at the town hall which carried a motion in favour of the railway line 'by a large majority.' [87] One meeting against the bill that did go ahead took place in Birmingham in April, when Riland Bedford successfully conscripted the supporting of leading figures from the town, including the influential minister George Dawson and Joseph Chamberlain, who was soon to become mayor. These men were anxious to preserve the park for the use of working people from Birmingham, and proved a useful source of subscriptions. George Dixon, one of the two MPs for Birmingham, set out the arguments against the railway line in the House of Commons. [88]

In the correspondence columns of the newspapers the Catholic priest John Buller Harkness let it be known that he thought that the proposed railway would result in 'an irreparable injury to the poor, especially of Sutton Coldfield' but undoubtedly the most powerful contribution came from A.W. Wills, a resident of Wylde Green who owned a works manufacturing edge tools in Birmingham, who set out in excruciating detail the links between the railway schemes and members or employees of the corporation:

'I ask you to let me state more explicitly than has yet been done some facts of grave importance … The solicitors to the … present scheme are Messrs.

---

[86] Ibid., 6 April 1872.

[87] Ibid.

[88] One Birmingham wag produced a mock placard for a public meeting (ibid., 1 April 1872): 'Notice. Calthorpe Park and Cannon Hill Park. The inhabitants of Sutton are requested to attend a public meeting at their town hall on April the first to make arrangements for the better government of the above parks in consequence of the people of Birmingham and their corporation being unable to mind their own business. Tee Ess Hee Warden.'

Sadler and Eddowes of Sutton Coldfield, the latter gentleman being warden of the corporation. The local agents to … Milward's line were Messrs. Holbeche and Addenbrooke, solicitors of Sutton Coldfield. The deputy stewards i.e. clerks and legal advisers of the corporation of Sutton are Messrs. Holbeche and Addenbrooke … Mr Addenbroke submitted the case … to Mr Clabon. It would be interesting to know in what terms the case was submitted inasmuch as the opinion of counsel generally depends mainly upon, and corresponds to, the manner in which the case is placed before him … it is questionable whether the gentleman occupying the double position of legal adviser to the corporation and land agent to the line, subsequently "rolled up" into the present scheme, was so far above the frailties of common human nature as to be precisely the proper person to conduct this part of the business … Now Mr Eddowes is an honourable man and held in high respect by all who know him, including myself … We do say … that he has been urged by his friends into a false position and one which has been fatal to the fair hearing of our side of the question; for mark the action of this (railway) committee … The constitution of this committee was simply monstrous and without parallel and that … rendered its action nugatory, futile – in fact a mockery.' [89]

The Mr Clabon referred to in this indignant letter was J.M. Clabon, a solicitor who specialised in advising on railway bills. The corporation had sought enlightenment from him and also from the land agents William Fowler and William Matthews. The recommendations that these three men offered were exactly what most members of the corporation wanted to hear: that the bill should not be opposed but refined with amendments. Members of the railway committee met frequently with the promotors of the railway, and, in March 1872, the bill was considered by a committee of the House of Commons. The deliberations extended over several days. The LNWR was the only voice of dissent - opponents of the scheme from Sutton were not present. Ironmasters and colliery owners explained why the railway was wanted, with the surveyor to the corporation Charles Cooper and the farmer 'old Mr Wiggan' being the only residents of Sutton to contribute. [90] Wiggan caused great hilarity by his observation that visitors 'coming along the road to the park with bands and banners were a great nuisance and frightened the

---

[89] Ibid., 1 April, 11 May 1872. The railway committee appointed by the corporation was made up of Eddowes, Bodington, Wiggan, Johnstone and Kittoe.
[90] Ibid., 26 June 1872.

life out of ... (his) horses.' [91] To no one's surprise the committee endorsed the aims of the bill.

In June 1872 the select committee of the House of Lords met. This time all of the interested parties were called – the promoters of the bill, which included the iron masters whose interests would be so well-served by the line, the LNWR which opposed it and those on either side from Sutton – and they were all represented by barristers. When the House of Commons committee assembled, Bodington was there, of course, to testify that the effect of the line on the park would be 'a slight injury only at two points ... hardly anything to speak of' and that the part of the park that would be affected was 'exceedingly boggy ... (and) not frequented by the people at all.' [92] John Wiggan reinforced this second point by observing that he had often seen 'a number of horses, cows and donkeys and other animals stuck in the mud ... the corporation servants dragged out the animals, some alive and some dead' [93] His evidence was summed up by a wag as saying that the railway 'would do the park no harm but on the contrary would fill up the bogs.' [94]

Amongst those who gave evidence on behalf of the opponents of the bill were Riland Bedford, Johnstone and Lloyd. Riland Bedford contended that the line 'would destroy the picturesqueness of the park and interfere with the enjoyment of those who frequented it'; Johnstone declared that 'the smoke and dirt coming from the railway would do away with the moral effect of the park as it existed at present ... he held that the power of the mind over the body was great when the former was influenced by the contemplation of pure nature'; and Lloyd observed that the ironmasters 'would like to have ... (the) railway ... but my contention is that it need not go through the park and that they could do very well without it.' [95] On the casting vote of the chairman Lord Camoys, the committee decided in favour of the promoters of the railway. The battle fought with such deep feeling had been lost. The

---

[91] Ibid., 19 March 1872.
[92] Ibid., 24 June 1872.

[93] Ibid.
[94] Ibid., 26 June 1872.
[95] Ibid., 25 June 1872.

railway across Sutton Park, with stations on the east and west sides, opened in August 1879. [96]

---

[96] See M. Hodder *The Archaeology of Sutton Park* (Stroud, 2013), pp. 150-2 for the route of the line.

## III: CRIME

*A view of Sutton c.1870*

On 30 December 1861 John Thompson of Sutton Coldfield was hanged for murder in front of the county gaol at Warwick. By this time only murderers were hanged, and most people believed that they deserved to be punished in this way. A crowd gathered outside the prison to witness proceedings, but was smaller than anticipated. Thompson was a wire drawer working in Aston and living in Sutton with Ann Walker, a married woman who had been estranged from her husband for several years and who he referred to as his housekeeper, and his five children. The couple had visited a fair in Birmingham on 28 September, staying overnight at a lodging house in Tanter Street, which was also known as a brothel. The next day they had gone out to visit a number of public houses, at one of which Walker had encountered a man with whom she had formerly co-habited. She returned inebriated to their lodging house, with Walker, who had also drunk too much, following soon after. An argument ensued in their room and, when Walker refused to return home to Sutton, Thompson cut her throat. At his trial at the Warwick Assizes in December Thompson's barrister, hastily pressed into service by the judge, called on the jury 'to give the poor man at the bar the same justice as they would extend to a person in a higher walk of life.' [97] But the judge made clear that he viewed this as nothing other than a case of murder and, after briefly considering the matter, the jury found Thompson guilty. A petition submitted to the Home Secretary Sir George

---

[97] *Aris's Birmingham Gazette,* 21 December 1861.

Grey by William Scholefield, one of the MPs for Birmingham, and Thompson's barrister was rejected.

Like other condemned men at this time, Thompson was encouraged to produce, or more likely agree to, a written confession. 'I hope my sad fate will be a warning to a great many of both sexes', he was said to have written. 'I am sorry I did it for I was very fond of her and she was a good, clean woman in the house.' [98] His statement included accusations of perjury by several witnesses who appeared at his trial, but concluded, 'I hope God will forgive them, as I do myself.' [99] Thompson was executed alongside another man, William Beamish, convicted of poisoning his wife. On the day of the execution the two men attended a service in the chapel before being pinioned and escorted to the scaffold. The executioner put on the caps, shook their hands 'and the bolt was at once withdrawn … (and) in a very short space of time they were dead; there was very little struggling.' [100] The bodies of the two men were buried within the precincts of the gaol. Within a few years public executions were brought to an end. This was believed to be a 'civilizing' step – but thereafter convicted men and women died alone, without the 'support' of the crowd. [101]

It was extremely rare for an inhabitant of Sutton Coldfield to be convicted of murder in the nineteenth century. Mostly, the crimes that the police constables and magistrates dealt with concerned drunk and disorderly behaviour and theft. Paid police constables arrived in Sutton as a result of the County and Borough Police Act 1856. Before then there had been an unpaid parish constable and, at night, elderly watchmen on patrol. Now the provision of full time police constables in every town became compulsory, and, in Sutton, these men were members of the Warwickshire Constabulary.

From census returns and newspaper reports we are able to put names to the police constables who patrolled the streets of Sutton. In 1871 there was Robert Norris, aged 41, who lived with his wife and five children in High Street. Typical of the tasks Norris undertook were the arrests of Charles Browne, also known as 'Fighter' Browne, and William Lakin for a breach

---

[98] Ibid., 4 January 1862.
[99] Ibid.
[100] Ibid.
[101] V.A.C. Gatrell, *The Hanging Tree: Execution and the English People 1770-1868* (Oxford, 1994) is a superb examination of this subject.

of the peace in Mill Street in April 1869; the two men were admonished and bound over for three months on sureties of £5 each by the magistrates. There was also PC Warren. During the Little Sutton Wake, in June 1871, he arrested, in a public house, William Jones 'who was drunk and behav(ing) in a most disgraceful way, almost stripping himself'; the magistrates fined Jones 40s.[102] Abel Smith was a sergeant, who had the responsibility of dealing with unlawful behaviour in Sutton Park. In 1881 the police constables included George Parry, aged 26, and James Brown, aged 19, both of whom lived in Mere Green; Thomas Turrell, aged 23, and living in lodgings; and Charles Churn, aged 34, and the father of three children. These men were supervised, for a time, by Superintendent Galloway, who sent his constables into the shops of bakers to catch out those who sold bread without proving its weight. It was a small police force, and, when large crowds arrived for the horse races in Sutton Park, large numbers of Birmingham police arrived with them. In the same year as the new arrangements for these constables were put in place, the corporation also sought to retain some local control by employing 'an active middle aged man to undertake the duties of a private policeman.' [103]

There was a police station in Sutton. Those who were due to appear before the magistrates were detained in the cells. By the mid-1870s it was agreed by the corporation that the conditions in which prisoners were held needed drastic improvement. The physician James Johnstone was shocked when he inspected the cells:

'There was no means of warming them in winter, water ran down the inside walls, and the bedding was in a most filthy state. The water closet was choked up, and there was no means of cleaning it, and altogether the condition of things was as bad as possible. He considered also that some provision should be made for the proper care of women who were locked up. At present a policeman could visit them and he did not think that was right. Again, under existing conditions, the prisoners were sometimes left alone in the cells for six, eight and ten hours at a stretch with no one in place.' [104]

---

[102] *Aris's Birmingham Gazette*, 17 June 1871.
[103] *Birmingham Journal*, 17 July 1858.
[104] *Birmingham Daily Post*, 13 June 1876.

Warned by Johnstone that a prisoner might commit suicide, the corporation agreed to improve the conditions in which prisoners were held and to seek to appoint a married police constable to live on the premises, with his wife caring for the females who had been detained.

Crimes of a minor nature which could be tried summarily were dealt with at the Petty Sessions in Sutton Coldfield before two magistrates or justices of the peace, one of whom was usually the warden. More serious crimes were sent by the process of indictment to be heard at the Quarter Sessions in Warwick before two or more magistrates sitting with a jury; the most serious crimes, those subject to capital punishment or life imprisonment, were sent for trial by judge and jury at the periodic Assizes. A person arrested by the constables might expect to be before the magistrates in a day or two. There were also private prosecutions. At these trials the magistrates did not dally as they worked through the cases before them. They had the power to impose short sentences of imprisonment on individuals they found guilty. Thus, in April 1869 Hannah Nichols was sent to gaol for seven days with hard labour for stealing coal; in September 1872 Thomas Stanley discovered that he would spend the next month in prison for stealing three sheaves of wheat; and in January 1874 James Moore found himself facing three months with hard labour for stealing a bed sheet off a washing line at Maney. Four men convicted of disorderly conduct at a public house in February 1869 were fined 6d each but 'being desirous of a change, they preferred a visit to Warwick.' [105] Even a boy who had stolen apples and gooseberries from the garden of the rector W.K. Riland Bedford was, in July 1871, sentenced to one day in the cells with the additional recommendation that his father severely admonish him. For the magistrates the defence of property was at the top of their list of priorities; those who sought to help themselves to another's property needed to face the full force of the law.

For all other offences the magistrates issued fines. Thus, Mrs Bird was fined 2s 6d and costs of 13s 6d in October 1867 for 'assaulting ... and calling her ... (neighbour Mrs Aspley) foul names'; Catherine Dudley was fined 1s in July 1870 for jumping out of a moving train at Chester Road station; and Abraham Grayer was fined £2 in August 1874 for selling beer without a licence. [106] And then there was the unfortunate Joseph Matthews who was fined 5s and costs in May 1873 for seeking to remove 71 ferns from Sutton

---

[105] *Birmingham Daily Gazette,* 1 February 1869.
[106] Ibid., 1 October 1867.

Park on the instructions of his employer James Adams of Parkfield House, Pershore Road, Birmingham. Collecting ferns was a passion for many Victorian gentleman. Adams was not arrested and therefore not present in court, although a clearly infuriated Riland Bedford did not hesitate to 'strongly censure ... (him) ... the real offender' and make clear 'his intention of punishing all future offenders with the utmost severity.' [107]

The protection of Sutton Park was a perpetual concern for the corporation. In July 1868 a fire, believed to have been started deliberately, destroyed over 500 acres of woodland; the smoke could be seen from as far away as Aston and people travelled by train to see what was happening. The corporation responded by offering the large sum of £100 for information leading to the arrest and conviction of any person who started a fire. At the Petty Sessions in November 1864 Henry Aubury, a spade maker, was fined 5s with damages of 6d and expenses of 16s 6d for cutting branches off an oak tree in the park. When it became clear that carts were being filled with holly during the nights as Christmas approached and then transported to Birmingham, the number of men paid to watch out for this was increased. At the Petty Sessions in November 1862 Joseph Bennett was fined 6d. plus damages for cutting off branches of holly trees in the park. The owners of private property also sought to defend their holly; at the Petty Sessions in February 1869 Edward Bills and Thomas Chambers were fined £2 each for stealing holly from a garden.

Cock fighting had been made illegal in 1849, but fights continued to be covertly arranged. A well-organised cock fight took place near to the Beggar's Bush on 17 April 1875, attended by about 40 onlookers, most of whom laid bets on the outcome. Warned by a look-out on horseback, these people immediately dispersed as police constables arrived. Edward Wilkinson and Richard Hadley, both cock trainers from Oldbury and Wednesfield respectively, and Edward Wright, a clerk from Oldbury, and a number of other men appeared before the magistrates at West Bromwich. The summons against several of these men, however, had not been taken out within the required month and they were discharged. The maximum fine of £5 was imposed on each of the defendants, with the magistrates expressing their regret that others involved had not been punished.

---

[107] *Birmingham Daily Post,* 3 May 1873.

The Quarter Sessions were held at Warwick in spring, summer, autumn and winter. Because the powers of magistrates in the Petty Sessions had been strengthened in 1848, fewer cases were being sent to Warwick. Violent assault, however, was one of them. This was not common in Sutton, but in March 1856 James Devine, Martin Ronan, Andrew Baker and Martin Diskin were sentenced to six months' imprisonment with hard labour for an assault on Thomas Faroner outside the Boot Inn. During the assault Devine falsely alleged that Faroner had stolen his horse and cart. 'They were all on me', Faroner testified, 'kicking me and beating me with stones. I was bruised all the way from the hip to the shoulders, up the back. I had a cut behind and on the top of the head.' [108] Poaching was another offence that took men to the Quarter Sessions – found guilty of the offence in March 1875, Henry Daniels spent the next six months in prison.

A case much talked-about locally also found its way to the Quarter Sessions in March 1872. In November 1870 the rector W.K. Riland Bedford had received an anonymous letter which informed him that 'he had better look out as he (the writer) should put a bullet in his head and blow up his house.' [109] Riland Bedford handed the letter to the Sutton police superintendent, but already had his suspicions about the identify of the author. He believed that it was Frederick Smith, a carpenter and a man he knew well but with whom he had recently had 'an angry conversation' and the behaviour of his dog.[110] At the Petty Sessions a letter written by Smith was produced and it was concluded that the handwriting resembled that in the threatening letter which the rector had received. So the matter was sent to the Quarter Assizes. Here a letter from Smith was produced in which he denied that he had written the threatening letter and that he had nothing but great respect for the rector. Riland Bedford, clearly keen to bring the matter to an end, declared that he believed Smith and a verdict of not guilty was returned.

It is worth noting that a few years earlier when Thomas Farmer, an agricultural labourer, threatened to kill his wife Elizabeth, he was not sent to the Quarter Assizes. It was reported that the 'complainant stated that her husband had frequently threatened to do some harm to her' and that, during

---

[108] *Aris's Birmingham Gazette,* 24 March 1856.
[109] *Birmingham Daily Post,* 28 January 1871.
[110] Ibid.

the trial, Farmer 'had nothing to say.' [111] Farmer was bound over to keep the peace for six months on two sureties of £10 each.

---

[111] *Birmingham Daily Gazette,* 11 May 1869. According to the census of 1871, Thomas and Elizabeth Farmer were still living together.

# IV: SCHOOLS

Elementary education for working class and lower middle class children had been provided across the town by the corporation since the mid-1820s. This had at first been free, but in due course weekly fees were introduced. Though the corporation paid for the building, maintenance and equipping of these schools and met, with only a small contribution from fees, the salaries of the schoolmasters and schoolmistresses, there was a very strong input into the day-to-day running by the Anglican clergymen of the parish. The day began with religious instruction - subsequently put back to later in the morning to ensure that late arrivals did not miss it – and the clergymen put in regular appearances. The schools were run in effect as if they were operated by the National Society, which funded the building of schools on behalf of the Church of England. There was no compulsion for parents to send their children to these schools. The weekly fees prevented the poor from doing so, though there was some provision for free admission if the parents could prove that they were unable to pay the fees. In 1874 the average daily attendance of boys at the town school was 86 and of girls 77.

Once a year the town school was visited by a government inspector. This would involve the inspector testing the abilities of the pupils in a range of subjects. The visit by William Scoltock in 1874 concluded that the school 'as a whole is making fair progress.' [112] There were 66 boys present on the day of inspection and of these 62 passed in reading, 62 in writing, 49 in arithmetic, 12 in geography and six in algebra. 'The children passed fairly in individual examinations', Scoltock observed, 'yet the teaching wants intelligence. Geography was very moderate and the arithmetic not well explained. Some attention should be paid to explanation of words in reading lessons.' [113] There were 55 girls present for their examination, with 51 passing in reading, 52 in writing, 34 in arithmetic, seven in geography and three in recitation. 'Reading of the first class good; of the second class fair; of the third and fourth classes good; many of the words explained in a satisfactory manner', Scoltock reported. [114] He also visited the infant school,

---

[112] *Birmingham Daily Post,* 12 January 1875.
[113] Ibid.
[114] Ibid.

run by Mary Groom and attended on average by 63 children. 'The children are kept in good order and clean', he noted. 'The instruction is well suited to them.'[115]

When an inspection in 1876 reported 'the numerous failures of scholars,' the corporation decided that an enquiry was required. [116] The schoolmaster George Preston and schoolmistress Marion Large were summoned to answer questions. Preston put these failings down to 'the boys not being sufficiently taught before they entered his school, partly to the thinness of the school for ten weeks and to the school being closed on account of scarlet fever. In the spring of the present year twenty eight boys had been absent each week.' [117] Large offered a similar explanation and these statements were accepted at the meeting of the corporation.

It would have been expected that clergymen from outside the parish would have inspected the town school and that lay inspectors did so suggests that the corporation had taken advantage of government grants that had been available since 1862. Yet it was reported in 1878 that the schools were operating at a loss of £400 per annum, 'a state of things it is impossible to contemplate the perpetuation of.' [118] A proposal to increase fees, according to age, from 1d to 3d a week, was rejected. The solution lay with a successful application for a government grant. When this was secured, the corporation decided, in March 1879, to end the payment of fees in its senior schools – except for those parents who offered to still pay them and for non-residents. To get onto the free list required 200 attendances a year, 250 if free clothing was also sought. One boy, in 1880, was denied free clothing when it was discovered that he was illegitimate. At a corporation meeting a furious A.W. Wills branded this 'an act of barbarism ... originally adopted for the protection of morality in the parish ... efficacious or not, it was highly unjust and unchristian.' [119] The policy remained in place. When any pupils on the free list failed to meet the required number of attendances, their parents were informed that fees were once again to be paid. A number refused and their children were suspended. This also provoked complaints at corporation

---

[115] Ibid.
[116] Ibid., 12 September 1876.
[117] Ibid.
[118] Ibid., 12 August 1878.
[119] Ibid., 14 December 1880.

meetings. The return of free schooling, however, saw the number of pupils increasing in the corporation schools – the total school population grew by 74 in 1879-80. This brought with it an increase in the government grant. At the six infant schools a weekly fee of £1 was still payable, raising £60 per annum for the corporation.

The expansion of numbers increased the work of the schoolmasters and schoolmistresses. In 1880 William Eden, the schoolmaster at Green Lanes, saw his salary increased by £12 – and his assistant replaced by a pupil teacher, saving £40 per annum. The greater number of pupils necessitated the erection of new school rooms. It was decided in 1879 that a new school room would be built at Hill for the boys, with the girls moving into the existing room. The new building at the infants school in Boldmere which was approved in 1881 would accommodate another 112 children at a cost of £450 - a decision not to include a new cloakroom saved £50. Meanwhile Riland Bedford decided to convert a barn owned by the corporation and used as a mission chapel at Whitehouse Common into a new infants school and appointed a schoolmistress – and suggested that the corporation take it over, an offer which it declined. By 1882 the corporation was boasting 'that expenditure per child was the highest of any town in the country with the exception of London.' [120] Yet for the barrister James Motteram, one of the most outspoken critics of the corporation in the town, that body was quite unfit to be running schools:

'He did not hesitate to say that they were utterly incapable of forming an opinion upon that subject ... Education, indeed. What did the corporation know about it? One them told him the other day that he hated their new-fangled scheme of education and that education had done nothing more for him than compelling him to pay 1s a day to a boy for frightening rooks when forty years ago 4d was the amount paid. The man who told him that might perhaps be able to write his own name, but it was doubtful if he could read it afterwards.' [121]

There was a Catholic school at the church in High Street, where Frances Walker was the schoolmistress. Sutton's Catholic priest J. B. Harkness, however, had seen corporation funds used to support Anglican schools in the

---

[120] Ibid., 13 December 1882.
[121] Ibid., 7 September 1875.

town and applied for a grant to open a school to serve the two Catholic congregations, mainly made up of Irish agricultural labourers. The corporation, however, refused this request. In February 1871 a petition, signed by 140 members of these congregations, requested that the corporation reconsider its decision, which they declared to be 'contrary to the expressed provisions of the charter, to the known feelings of the founders of the charity and to the unquestionable claims of the Roman Catholic inhabitants of the parish.' [122] These arguments did not impress the members of the corporation. In language which reflected his anti-Irish and anti-Catholic prejudices, John Wiggan observed that the petition 'purported to have been signed by the inhabitants of a row of cottages and these persons could not write a legible hand and he did not believe they could read. They were only common labourers who could not understand the memorial'. [123] Only one member of the corporation was prepared to support the scheme – George Bodington.

There were many private schools, taking middle class girls and boys as both day pupils and boarders, in Sutton. Mary and Elizabeth Birch, both unmarried, ran a school at Maney House, owned by their mother. In 1851 they were employing an assistant Mary Dunkley and there were eleven girls in residence. In July 1859 the school re-located to Frederick Street in Edgbaston. A new school was opened in Maney House by three unmarried sisters, Mary, Ellen and Harriet Todd. In 1871 they were employing Lucy Dixon to teach English and Aline Steed to teach French, and had ten girls, aged between ten and fifteen, in residence. As an alternative, Grace Sturland, who hailed from Ashby-de-la-Zouch, and the Misses Bavington ran the Ashby House Ladies School on the Dam and Mrs William Wadhams – formerly Miss Clues - presided over the Sutton Coldfield Establishment for Young Ladies. Some middle class Suttonians still preferred to employ governesses to teach their children at home. [124]

J.C. Cull ran, with his wife, the Preparatory School for Young Gentleman in High Street. This catered for pupils up to twelve, both day boys and

---

[122] Ibid., 15 February 1871.
[123] Ibid.
[124] See *Birmingham Daily Gazette,* 26 December 1870 for an advertisement for 'a daily governess of the Church of England to instruct young children in English, French and music.'

boarders. Richard Holbeche, a member of a well-known local family, remembered his time there:

'When I first went to their academy, there was a little school room looking down the yard or playground, but, during my career there and as the school became more prosperous, it was very much enlarged ... Mr Cull had a pupil, Charley Perkins, I should say about eighteen years of age at that time. He said he was "reading" with Mr Cull. He did read a novel a little, in an armchair and got up at intervals to spit out of the window, which was all very fine and impressive ... Mrs Cull, a kind, motherly woman, did most of the teaching, helped by Miss Craven ... I have often reflected that I could not have greatly distinguished myself at this school for the only prize I received was one for "gentlemanly conduct in the school room". I fancy it must have perplexed good Mr Cull to find out even this virtue ... Mr Cull was churchwarden for many years and was generally a useful man in town matters. A really good fellow and a character.' [125]

In 1853, after eight years in the role, Matthew Wilson's time as headmaster of the town school came to an end and he opened Park House Classical and Commercial School at Doe Bank, a gentleman's house in Four Oaks. Within two years, owing to an increase in the number of pupils, Wilson re-located his establishment, which became the Anchorage House Classical and Commercial School. Wilson's staff included Herr Lampert as professor of German and music, R. Mills as drawing master and Monsieur Alfred Gilmer in charge of calisthenics – a form of gymnastic exercise - dancing, fencing and drill. As if he did not already have enough on his plate, Gilmer expanded his activities to include classes in dancing for adults and children on Friday evenings. According to the census returns, Wilson was accommodating fifteen boarders in 1861. There was another move in 1871 and Wilson now installed himself as principal of Ashfurlong Hall Classical and Commercial School, set in 56 acres. Monsieur Gilmer was still with him, though his responsibilities had been reduced to calisthenics and dancing – with W. Murphy as senior master, Mr Wadhams as junior master, and Monsieur Perret teaching French and drawing. Unlike the masters at the grammar school, these men did not have degrees. Matthew Wilson, who played a

---

[125] sclhrg.org.uk/images/stories/transcriptions/My-Recollections-of-Sutton-Coldfield. pdf pp. 6-7.

prominent part in the public affairs of Sutton, died in Handsworth in August 1891, leaving a very small estate.

In summer 1865 advertisements appeared in local newspapers advertising the opening of Clyde House School, with Robert de Lisle Smith, who had taught at Cull's school, as headmaster. The school was located on the Dam, in a house owned by the farmer Joseph Dutton. A full range of subjects would be taught and fees of between 35 and 50 guineas would be charged, depending on age. And then, almost out of nowhere, Smith found himself embroiled in controversy. It was revealed that he was the author of a letter which sought contributions towards the purchase of an annuity of £35 to £40 for a widow who was suffering from paralysis and had the care of five children under ten. The letter gave the impression that the author was a clergyman – he referred to 'my parish' - and gave Sutton Coldfield as his address. [126] The recipient passed the letter to Riland Bedford and the warden Thomas Colmore was asked to investigate. At first Smith tried to brazen it out. He declared that the widow lived in Dalkeith - 'where I am well known' - but did not respond to requests from Colmore for her name or address; it was soon established that no woman in this situation could be traced in that town. [127] Sarah Holbeche had no doubts that Smith's appeal was 'purely an invention to help himself.' [128] Smith himself disappeared and Clyde House School never opened; the last we hear of him is Dutton demanding that he remove his furniture and possessions from the house he had rented.

Bishop Vesey's Grammar School was emerging from a period in the doldrums. Charles Barker, who during his tenure as headmaster had managed to reduce the number of pupils to one, had died suddenly as he returned on horseback from a visit to Penns Hall in October 1842 and his successor James Eccleston had lasted for only five years, compelled to resign as his debts mounted. With the appointment of Josiah Wright in July 1849, however, the school began to make progress. [129] Aged twenty five, Wright was a man of scholarly inclinations and, having been encouraged by his tutor

---

[126] *Birmingham Daily Post*, 25 August 1865.
[127] Ibid.
[128] sclhrg.org.uk/research/transcriptions/2536-sarah-holbeche-diary.html?start=61, 25 August 1865, p. 80.
[129] For a full account of the grammar school during these years see K. Osbourne, *A History of Bishop Vesey's Grammar School: The First 375 Years* (Sutton Coldfield, 1990), pp. 141-272.

at Trinity Hall, Cambridge, W.H. Thompson, he arrived at the school with published translations of three works by Plato already to his name. He was subsequently to bring out *The Seven Kings of Rome,* an abridged version of the first book of Livy's history of Rome with very extensive notes, and *David, King of Israel* (1860), based on lectures he gave at the school during daily bible readings and described by one magazine as 'exceedingly valuable … a most useful gift book for the young.' [130] At the time he was appointed as headmaster of the grammar school, he was earning his living as a private tutor of classics. The school was to become a family home – Wright married Jane Govett in April 1852 and their three children were born there.

Wright was assisted, as second master, by the Revd. Thomas Suter Ackland, who taught mathematics, and by Mr Bray, who taught English. Ackland was paid a salary of £100 per annum, topped up with a share of the school fees – but, from this, he had to contribute £5 to Bray's salary of £20 per annum. Like Wright, he was able to supplement his income by taking in boarders – in his case in a rented house in the High Street. [131] He was succeeded in 1853 by Richard Yeld, whose three sons attended the school. In due course Yeld found himself involved in a legal action by a parent relating to the frequency of his caning. Yeld prevailed and 'was pulled by the boys in a carriage on his return from court in triumph' but, unsurprisingly, resigned soon after. [132] It seems that Wright was left to get on with running the school unhindered. Attendance at meetings of the governors was invariably very small; indeed one governor did not attend a single meeting and another explained he was unable to attend a meeting because he had a 'pressing engagement which I much wish to keep' – he was in fact going hunting. [133]

The clergymen who paid annual visits to inspect the school were always impressed by the standard of the boys' work. In December 1855 the Revd. R. G. Latham reported that 'those boys who had been there any length of time answered extremely well in arithmetic'; and in classics the Revd. R. W.

---

[130] *Lady's Own Paper,* 29 December 1860. Also see *Evening Mail,* 21 January 1856, for a review of Wright's *A Help to Latin Grammar* which declared, 'No child of moderate capacity can fail to understand this grammar, the study of which ought to precede that of every other.'

[131] T.S. Ackland died in May 1892, leaving only £299 1s 6d.

[132] sclhrg.org.uk/images/stories/transcriptions/My-Recollections-of-Sutton-Coldfield.pdf. p. 15.

[133] Quoted in K. Osbourne, *A History of Bishop Vesey's Grammar School,* p. 165.

Essington observed that he had 'rarely, if ever, heard boys translate so lucidly and effectively.' [134] All of this for fees declared to be 'nominal' and 'very moderate.' [135] The number of pupils began to increase – there were fourteen when Wright took up the post and thirty two ten years later. At one point there were eighteen boarders. The eventual destinations of the boys was advertised as being public schools, military colleges and the civil service.

Wright's plans for improvement included the establishment of a library – for which he solicited subscriptions – and the building of substantial new accommodation. These buildings would include a school room and a significant expansion of the dormitories, in an attempt to recruit more boarders and thereby increase his own income. It seems that the new buildings, which were finished in April 1861, were financed by a loan from a wealthy relation of Wright's. But still the boarders did not come in the numbers Wright hoped for and, in summer 1863, he resigned. He left all his furniture and the contents of his garden – ranging from 'a gentleman's wardrobe in the best Spanish mahogany' to eleven tons of manure – behind him and these were sold off at an auction. [136] Wright re-located to St. Leonards-on-Sea in Sussex, where he took holy orders, becoming a curate at St. Mary Magdalen's Church and the proprietor of Barnham House, a private school. He died in June 1898, leaving £9,725.

To become headmaster of Bishop Vesey's Grammar School was to secure a prestigious position, locally and beyond. The vacancy was advertised in newspapers across the country, and there were a large number of applications, a mixture of second masters and existing headmasters. The Revd. Albert Smith of Lincoln College, Oxford, and subsequently of King Edwards School, Birmingham, was appointed.[137] Smith appears to have been a well-respected, likeable man: he was to occupy the post for the next

---

[134] *Birmingham Journal,* 22 December 1855. These men were clearly well-known to Wright, Latham being vice-master of his old college.
[135] *Aris's Birmingham Gazette,* 20 July 1850, 21 July 1856. Most of the pupils lived in Sutton and the fees charged were ten shillings a quarter.
[136] Ibid., 18 July 1863.
[137] See *Birmingham Journal,* 29 December for a full list of the masters at King Edwards, where Smith's name follows that of the headmaster E.H. Gifford and he is described as 'headmaster's assistant.'

thirty nine years. In 1871 he was living at the school with his wife Frances, two sons and daughter and two boarders.

*The tomb of Bishop Vesey, Holy Trinity*

When Smith arrived, there were 29 pupils in the school – within two years the numbers had increased to 51 and in 1876 reached 115. The pupils studied Latin (and some of them Greek), theology, arithmetic, history, geography, grammar, composition and literature, a foreign language, and drawing. They were divided into classes according to ability – the top class consistently impressing in the annual examination but the lower classes not usually acquitting themselves particularly well and, in 1868, being described as 'hav(ing) a larger average than usual of dull boys ...' [138] Smith entered the most able boys for the Oxford and Cambridge Local Examinations, which they sat in Birmingham and provided a route into the universities. We find J.B. Cull, J.H. Davis and H.C. Hill particularly distinguishing themselves in 1867 and 1869. Cull, the son of the local schoolmaster J.C. Cull, went on to Balliol College, Oxford and, from 1878 to 1881, was headmaster of Colombo Academy in Ceylon. Smith was supported by a succession of masters. Generally these men stayed for only a few years. The Rev. F.A. Goddard was appointed the second master in 1866; an applicant for the headmastership three years earlier, he waited eleven years for Smith to move

---

[138] Quoted in K. Osbourne, *A History of Bishop Vesey's Grammar School,* p. 199.

on before he did so himself. He was later succeeded by the Revd. O.A. Archer.

During these years sport began to play a more important role in the life of the grammar school than it had hitherto. There was an annual sports day in which boys competed in such activities as throwing the cricket ball and the hammer, the high jump and flat, hurdle and sack races, the latter of which 'caused much amusement.' [139] These were well-attended events. 'The weather was by no means favourable – a raw, cold wind prevailed during the whole of the afternoon', it was reported. 'The friends of the athletes mustered, however, in strong forces.' [140] Smith also arranged cricket matches, invariably opening the batting for the school himself; in July 1870, in a match against Oscott College's second team, he was dismissed for a duck.

The grammar school was, after the parish church, the most significant institution in Sutton. Smith, like his predecessors, was invited to become a member of the corporation. He became chairman of the schools attendance committee and also addressed public meetings on issues of local concern. For example, in 1868, he supported a campaign to open a bathing pool in Sutton Park. He was very much a public figure, recognised by many of the inhabitants. The sons of most of the prominent families in the town – the Bodingtons, the Chavasses, the Holbeches and so on - were pupils at the school. [141] There was a concern, expressed at meetings and in memorials, that the school curriculum was not suitable for preparing those boys who would enter commerce, and, during tortuous discussions that took place for several years after 1875 regarding the role to be played by the corporation in the reorganisation and enlargement of the school, it must at times have seemed to Smith that almost every inhabitant of the town had an opinion. [142]

It was not until 1882 that new arrangements were put in place regarding such matters as the number of governors, the size of the staff, the curriculum, fees and salaries. Smith expressed himself delighted with the interest the boys

---

[139] *Birmingham Daily Gazette,* 28 April 1870.
[140] *Birmingham Daily Post,* 5 May 1871.
[141] Oliver Bodington 1867-72, Thomas Chavasse 1864-5, Richard Holbeche 1861-5, amongst many others. I am grateful to Kerry Osbourne for this information.
[142] See W.K. Riland Bedford, *History of Sutton Coldfield,* p. 65 for a summary of the issues at stake.

showed in their new lessons in chemistry, but was disappointed by progress in singing which he attributed to the obstacle that 'a good many boys … either are unable, or think themselves unable, to sing at all.' [143]

---

[143] Quoted in K. Osbourne, *A History of Bishop Vesey's Grammar School,* p. 255.

# V LEISURE

The Sutton Coldfield Institute and Reading Room came into existence in autumn 1853. It proved to have a long life. It grew out of a subscription library founded with the support of the rector Richard Williamson in the 1840s. His successor W.K. Riland Bedford played a leading role in the new venture, which, like its predecessor, arranged public lectures at the the town hall. These lectures encompassed history, literature and science. Riland Bedford himself gave a lecture on the English long bow, on which he became a self-taught expert. He also invited his friends the Revd. E. Harston of Tamworth and the Revd. E. Spooner of Birmingham to offer their thoughts about, respectively, popular literature and the poetry of Sir Walter Scott.

To draw larger audiences the programme was given a make-over. Public readings from novels and plays became increasingly popular in the third quarter of the nineteenth century. And so the Institute began to arrange such readings. James Bennett, a retired actor from the Theatre Royal in Birmingham, offered the *The Merchant of Venice,* and the Revd. E.H. Kittoe read one of the cantos from Scott's *Marmion.* It was, however, readings from Dickens' *Pickwick Papers* or his Christmas stories by the schoolmaster J.H. Cull or the solicitor T.S. Eddowes, together with extracts from that collection of myths and ghost stories much-loved by the Victorians, R.H. Barham's *The Ingoldsby Legends,* read by the Revd. J. Downs of Stonnall that proved most popular. Readings lasted 20-30 minutes and were interspersed with songs. Gone were lectures on slavery in America: this was light entertainment.

These readings attracted large attendances of middle class Suttonians. Only in the 1860s did members of the Institute attempt to attract working class people. This was done by a series of readings which could be heard on payment of one penny. At one gathering the chairman 'alluded to the usefulness of these amusements in elevating the ideas of the lower classes …' [144] In March 1864 the Revd. Kittoe read 'very humorously' from *Nicholas Nickleby*; in November 1866 J.A. Langford, a poet and antiquarian from Birmingham, read Tennyson's 'The Northern Farmer' and 'the

---

[144] *Birmingham Daily Gazette,* 4 December 1867.

admirable rendering of the dialect amused the audience not a little'; and in December 1866 the celebrated preacher from the Church of the Saviour in Birmingham George Dawson read extracts from *Vanity Fair* by William Makepeace Thackeray. [145] Intended to be both 'highly instructive and amusing', these events also included the singing of comic songs; so enjoyable was the performance of Birmingham tailor William Joyce Page in November 1866 that he was called back for encores.[146]

There was still a place for public lectures in the small intellectual world of nineteenth century Sutton. After he had spent 1882 on a lecture tour of the United States, the playwright and poet Oscar Wilde embarked, in the second half of 1883, on a lecture tour of Britain, describing his impressions of the country. He arrived in Sutton that September. Dressed soberly and not in the flamboyant velvet coat and knee breeches for which he was known, he expanded on railways in the US (the steam whistles and newspaper boys greatly annoyed him), the constant hurry that people appeared to be in and the odd names of some towns. The journalists present pronounced the lecture 'decidedly interesting', but the reaction of Wilde's audience was one 'of cold curiosity.' [147]

The members of the Institute also put on a number of dramatic performances. At Christmas 1867 a series of comic sketches was performed at the town hall, and 'Mr Poole excited much risibility by his personation of the Hon. Augustus Collander Yawn.' [148] The proceeds of the event went towards funding a soup kitchen. There was another successful display of amateur dramatics at the town hall the following Christmas, with the Institute the

---

[145] Ibid., 24 March 1864, 21 November, 4 December 1867; sclhrg.org.uk/research/transcriptions/2536-sarah-holbeche-diary.html, 2 December 1865, p. 84 for Sarah Holbeche's verdict on Dawson's reading: 'too course for his warmest admirers'; also see ibid., 23 October 1865, p. 83 for a visit to Sutton by Dawson in October 1865 when he 'lectured on the days of Good Queen Bess – very clever and new – making the execution of Mary a necessity not a choice?'
[146] *Birmingham Daily Gazette*, 21 November 1866; 28 November 1867.
[147] *Birmingham Daily Post,* 2 October 1883.
[148] Ibid., 2 January 1868. The Hon. Augustus Collander Yawn is a character in John Courtney's comedy *Time Tries All!*

beneficiary. By the 1880s the town hall was being used three times a year for theatrical performances.

The members of the Institute all had access to the reading room and were able to borrow books. They were, however, also purchasers of books. In the homes of the middle class in Sutton the works of Scott, Dickens and Tennyson and others would have been found. A book which many of them also acquired was *History of the Forest and Chase of Sutton Coldfield,* which was brought out by in August 1860 by Simpkin & Marshall, a London publisher who expected the authors to pay the printing costs. Painstakingly researched and fluently written, this volume, like many similar books of the time, set the local story within an often-detailed national account. The author was not identified, but it soon became known in Sutton that the book had been written by Agnes Bracken. Unmarried and living with her mother and sisters in a comfortable house in the High Street, Bracken was unquestionably talented, spending her time absorbed in music, drawing and writing. There were now also local weekly newspapers to read – the *Sutton Coldfield and Erdington News* and the *Sutton Coldfield and Erdington Times*

The cricket club continued to thrive. The season began in June and ran until September, with matches between members of the club commencing at 4.30 pm every Wednesday and Friday at Rectory Park. The annual subscription was five shillings, and many of the professional men of the town were involved. For example, in the 1860s the secretary was C.J. Riland Bedford, the brother of the rector W.K. Riland Bedford, and the treasurer was the schoolmaster Matthew Wilson. It was the secretary who arranged matches against other clubs – such as Curdworth, Atherstone and the Free Foresters - and sent reports to the newspapers. Thus we read, in August 1858, of the teams of Sutton and Aston breaking for 'a substantial lunch' in the middle of the match; in August 1863, of 'Mr Kempson's shooters making sad havoc with the Cannock wickets'; and, in August 1871, of the secretary playing for Hams Hall 'who profited considerably by his steady fielding.' [149]

When the Sutton cricketers played another club 'the number of visitors was large, including a goodly number of ladies.' [150] These matches were,

---

[149] Ibid., 30 August 1858; *Birmingham Journal,* 30 May 1863; *Birmingham Daily Gazette,* 8 August 1871.
[150] *Birmingham Daily Post,* 20 August 1858.

however, very much recreation for the middle class. A sporting event that attracted considerably more spectators and from across the social spectrum was the steeplechase which took place in Sutton Park at the beginning of each year. It was far more than a local event, attracting bookmakers from as far away as London and 'many of the best steeplechase horses in the kingdom.' [151] There were several races each day, with purses of between 40 sovereigns (the Maiden Hunt Plate) and 100 sovereigns (the Erdington Plate). 'The weather was exceedingly fine, the ground in admirable condition, the attendance numerous and the sport ... quite of average quality', it was reported of the event in February 1862. [152] Many people walked from Birmingham to the park and 'heavily laden trains were despatched with great rapidity' from New Street. [153] Such large crowds needed to be heavily policed. In 1857 the police constables of Sutton and Birmingham were strengthened by the enrolment of 50 special constables.

Flat racing also took place in Sutton Park. In summer 1868 a new race course was opened 'at considerable expense' by John Sheldon near Westwood Coppice. [154] Being much softer soil, it was better site than the now-disused race course at Holly Knoll. In shape the course was oval and extended to one-and-a-quarter miles. Six races took place each day, which could be watched from a grandstand erected under the supervision of the corporation surveyor or from gentle elevations surrounding the course. Huge numbers of people travelled on the railway to Sutton, greatly upsetting many of the inhabitants. In August 1879 the journey from New Street was made 'absolutely repugnant by the disgusting exhibition of almost half-naked boys, who were attired Zulu fashion, and begged coppers from the passers-by for throwing Catherine wheels in the road.' [155] There were confrontations between race goers too. In July 1868 Samuel Haughton was compelled to issue a public apology when he accused the trainers of R.

---

[151] *Birmingham Journal,* 7 March 1857.
[152] *Aris' Birmingham Gazette,* 2 March 1861.
[153] *Birmingham Journal,* 15 February 1868.
[154] Ibid., 4 July 1868; see M. Hodder, *The Archaeology of Sutton Park* (Stroud, 2013), pp. 146-7.
[155] *Birmingham Daily Post,* 20 August 1879. The Zulu War was taking place in South Africa at this time.

Douglas Lane's horse 'in the most abusive terms' of having tampered with the saddlecloths. [156]

The race course at Westwood Coppice closed in 1879, but a few years later a new course was opened by John Sheldon jnr. in Four Oaks Park. It offered both flat races and steeplechases. Attendances were often 'enormous' - it was estimated that on one day in June 1881 about 20,000 people travelled to Four Oaks Park from Birmingham and the Black Country.[157] A large number of police were deployed at these races, and operated a temporary lock-up. Inevitably they were kept busy: in October 1881 George Richards, a bookmaker, assaulted two police officers and, with previous convictions for assault and pick pocketing, subsequently found himself sentenced to two months in prison with hard labour.

*The popular recreation of boating on Wyndley Pool*

The pools in Sutton Park offered boating, fishing and refreshments. These operations were run by men who had paid for licences from the corporation. In the early 1860s Charles James Phillips, who owned a hotel in New Street in Birmingham, kept a large number of boats and offered season tickets for fishing at Wyndley Pool 'which has not been fished for forty years.' [158] He subsequently leased Blackroot Pool 'and had the water weeds cut and the

---

[156] *Birmingham Daily Gazette,* 6 August 1868.
[157] *Birmingham Mail,* 29 May 1882.
[158] *Birmingham Daily Gazette,* 28 April 1863.

pool cleansed and the fishing is reported to be first rate.' [159] In the late 1860s John Knibb of Wylde Green was the proprietor of Wyndley and Powell's Pools. In the winter, he sought to attract skaters to Wyndley, which he described as 'the finest board of ice in the midland counties; smooth, safe and well preserved.'[160] Those who wanted to engage in shooting and coursing in the park also obtained licences from the corporation. They often also owned estates in which they could indulge in these activities. The wire manufacturer Baron D. Webster regularly shot ducks on his estate at Penns. After his death his business partner James Horsfall bought Penns Hall, choosing not to live there but keeping his greyhounds there so that, when he visited, he could go out coursing on his estate.

To the consternation of many Suttonians – though not the shopkeepers and particularly not the publicans – a new venture began to attract large numbers of visitors to the town. In summer 1868 Job Cole, well-known locally as a plantsman, opened the Royal Promenade Gardens adjacent to the main gate of Sutton Park. An annual subscription could be purchased, but most visitors entered by paying the day rate of 2d. Cheap excursion trains from New Street were put on and visits to these gardens and the park made Sutton an appealing day out. Cole turned ten uncultivated acres into gardens of great beauty – he planted lines of yews and limes around the edges of the gardens, laid down lawns, created gravel paths and made roses the central feature. Within a few years he was boasting that there were 20,000 rose bushes. There were also picnic areas, refreshments, a bowling green, a croquet lawn, and, eventually, a small hotel. In summer 1876 a staggering 110,000 people visited the gardens, 77,500 of them arriving on excursion trains.

*The hotel and crystal palace near to the main entrance of Sutton Park*

---

[159] Ibid.,, 10 April 1871.
[160] *Aris's Birmingham Gazette,* 4 December 1869.

In 1878 the newly-formed Sutton Park Crystal Palace and Aquarium Company entered into a business arrangement with Cole to rebuild the hotel so that it could accommodate 600 people and also provide a winter garden, a ball and concert room, a skating rink and, underneath an iron and glass dome, an aquarium. It was noticeable that of the seven directors of the new company only one – John McClelland – was a Sutton Coldfield man. Investors were promised a dividend of 25%, but within a few years the company had got into financial difficulties and went into liquidation.

Many of the gentlemen of Sutton took a great interest in their gardens. They oversaw the creation of their gardens, deciding what should be planted and where – though they themselves did not actually do much planting, weeding or cutting back, preferring to leave that to their gardeners.

The Sutton Coldfield Floral and Horticultural Society was established in 1859 with the purpose of organising an exhibition each summer over one, and sometimes two, days, usually in Sutton Park. To be admitted to the exhibition, visitors had to pay a fee of 1s, reduced to 6d in the evening. There were displays of roses, dahlias, pansies, ferns, fruit and vegetables in several tents, and the gentlemen's gardeners, nurserymen, amateurs and cottagers competed for money prizes and silver cups. With the exception of those who occupied the cottages owned by the corporation, exhibitors did not need to live in Sutton. The gentlemen were competitive and it was a source of considerable local prestige when their exhibits won prizes – it was, for example, a good day for Edwin Wright of Erdington in August 1859 when his gardener James Hodges secured the two main prizes for greenhouse plants and ornamental foliage. In summer 1882, in the fruit section, the Earl of Shrewsbury swept all before him for his grapes, melons, peaches and strawberries; amongst the cottagers the black currants were deemed 'very fine' but the raspberries were 'a poor show.' [161]

The public houses of Sutton were always busy, but particularly so on Sundays in summer when large numbers of people arrived from Birmingham to visit the park. George Bunn was, for many years, the licensee of the Cup – the inn was owned by the corporation – and he cultivated this trade by placing advertisements in the Birmingham newspapers informing readers of his dinners at 5 pm on Sundays and the times the omnibuses ran, 'giving

---

[161] *Birmingham Daily Post,* 20 July 1882.

ample time for refreshment and a stroll in Sutton Park.' [162] Thomas Bond, the landlord of the Horse and Jockey, meanwhile, sought to attract the custom of those who planned to stay overnight in Sutton; he described himself as a hotel keeper. Charles Atkins ran a beer house in Sadler Street. In about 1859 he moved his business across the road to what had been a private residence, built in 1853, but seemingly not lived in, for the Sutton-born jockey John Wells. Like its predecessor, this drinking establishment was known as the Duke and its location in due course became known as Duke Street. Adkins remained the licensee until his death in 1880, when his wife Eliza took over. [163] Public houses like the Duke, the Gate and the Boot were at the heart of working class life in the town. The licensees of public houses found themselves subject to the Licensing Act 1872, which restricted opening hours – closing time was now 11 pm – and sought to prevent the adulteration of beer, particularly with salt. The Sutton landlords and the working men who enjoyed a pint in these pubs were not best pleased by the stricter opening hours. [164]

The Three Tuns 'solicit(ed) the favour of the nobility, gentry and public at large' and, with five parlours, was able to ensure that they did not meet. [165] Bedrooms could be rented on a long-term basis and men like Frederick Wallis, who died at the inn in June 1862, had made it their home. In 1855 Harry Smith, proprietor of the Three Tuns for forty five years, decided to retire. The inn was 'now doing a capital commercial, general tavern and posting business' and was sold to E.M. Davis for about £600. [166] A few years later James Davy took over. He offered 'a first class lunch' and also providing refreshments at events organised by local societies. [167] Dinners remained an important source of income – the Sutton Tories always

---

[162] *Birmingham Journal,* 11 July 1857. Subsequently Joseph Clibbery was the licensee at the Cup, living there with his wife, four sons, daughter and daughter-in-law in 1871.
[163] I am grateful to Yvonne Moore for sharing with me her research on the history of the Duke.
[164] See *Birmingham Daily Post,* 9 May 1862 for a report of a meeting of the Sutton Coldfield Total Abstinence Society.
[165] *Aris's Birmingham Gazette,* 14 April 1856.
[166] Ibid., 7 May 1855.
[167] *Birmingham Daily Gazette,* 18 July 1864.

celebrated the return of their candidates in general elections at the Three Tuns.

*The Three Tuns*

The face of Sutton was changing. With the streets of the town very busy in the summer months, new hotels opened. In 1859 William Giles left the Waggon and Horses Inn in Handsworth to become the tenant of the Railway Hotel in the High Street, formerly a town house. The hotel - known to Suttonians as Giles' Hotel - became a focal point for local activities – auctions of livestock, land and furniture were held there and it was the meeting place for the South Staffordshire Hounds. To promote the hotel and its gardens Giles decided to commission a series of engravings from William Hawkins. According to Hawkins, Giles declared himself 'quite delighted' and his wife 'quite in ecstasy' when the engravings delivered, but then changed his mind 'and ... got into a savage temper and refused to pay ...' In a subsequent legal case Giles was ordered to pay the £2 he had agreed for the engravings. [168] The hotel was sold to a new owner in March 1864 for £5,060. In 1869 its name was changed to the Swan, with Giles employing three live-in staff. [169]

With the arrival of the railway, it seemed an excellent commercial project to investors from Birmingham to build a new hotel. This was the Royal Hotel,

---

[168] Ibid., 10 December 1863.
[169] This hotel should not be confused with an inn of the same name near to the grammar school – and known as the top Swan to differentiate it.

which opened on a site of two-and-a-half acres in May 1865. [170] On a high elevation with views of the park, this 'handsome Gothic structure' was intended to be a prestigious establishment. [171] The 'lofty' dining room could accommodate seventy people and there was a billiard room, a smoking room and separate coffee rooms for gentlemen and ladies. [172] The superior rooms included a piano. The first of a series of unsuccessful managers was J.J. Short. He was succeeded by a Mrs Green and then by Emma Clisby, who employed eleven live-in staff, including a bookkeeper, a billiard master, a cab driver, a cook and two laundresses. The Royal Hotel was expected to be 'a decided success', but it did not have enough capital behind it and debts began to mount up. [173] Sarah Holbeche was not in the least surprised by the difficulties the hotel soon ran into: 'short run indeed – who would have expected it. Everybody who could say 2+2 are 4', adding a fortnight later 'Hotel difficulties much; and by no means tenderly talked about.' [174] There was talk of the hotel being bought and used as a training college by the Methodists or turned into a sanatorium. George Bodington led the opposition to the second proposal and sought to gather investors to buy and re-open the hotel. The hotel had cost £14,000 to build and an additional £1,500 had been expended on furniture. Bodington's plan and then another scheme to buy the hotel came to nothing, but eventually it was sold for £9,000 to a company set up by, amongst others, the solicitor T.S. Eddowes and Henry Allbutt of the Midland Land & Investment Company. Under new ownership, the Royal Hotel re-opened in January 1869. It boasted hot water to all rooms and the dining room was 'fitted up in a style of great elegance', but was never to be a commercial success. [175] When C. Showell and J.H. Wilkinson of Showell's Brewery Company bought the hotel in 1889, they agreed a price of only £6,000, with an additional £2,000 for the furniture. The hotel was let to Emile Chatrian and then turned over without an exchange of money to become a sanatorium for 'respectable' working people such as clerks, shop assistants. The sanatorium opened in May 1896 and, nominated by a subscriber, residents were limited to staying for one

---

[170] This building in King Edward Square later became the Council House and is now converted into apartments.
[171] *Aris' Birmingham Gazette,* 16 January 1869.
[172] *Birmingham Daily Gazette,* 25 May 1865.
[173] *Aris's Birmingham Gazette,* 20 May 1865.
[174] sclhrg.org.uk/research/transcriptions/2536-sarah-holbeche-diary.html?start=64, 2, 15 December 1865, p 84.
[175] *Aris's Birmingham Gazette,* 16 January 1869.

week only, paying 10s 6d. The early expectations that investors in the Royal Hotel would enjoy handsome dividends were never realised. [176]

---

[176] Ibid. With the closure of the Royal Hotel in King Edward Square, the Swan Hotel (formerly the Railway Hotel) in the High Street changed its name to the Royal Hotel, which is the name it was known as for well over a century until new owners changed it again to the Town House in 2019.

## About the Author

Stephen Roberts holds honorary positions as Associate Professor and as a Fellow at, respectively, the Australian National University and the University of Birmingham. He is also a Fellow of the Royal Historical Society. He is the author or editor of books about both Chartism and Victorian Birmingham.

Selections from the Birmingham Biographies Series:

*Sir Benjamin Stone 1838-1914: Photographer, Traveller and Politician* (2014), £5.02

*Sir Richard Tangye 1833-1906: A Cornish Entrepreneur in Victorian Birmingham* (2015), £4.99

*Joseph Chamberlain's Highbury: A Very Public Private House* (2015), £3.99

*Joseph Gillott and Four Other Birmingham Manufacturers* (2016), £6.99

*Birmingham 1889: One Year in a Victorian City* (2017), £4.99

*Recollections of Victorian Birmingham* (2018), £4.99

*Webster & Horsfall & the Atlantic Cable* (2020), £4.50

*George Dawson & the Church of the Saviour* (2020), £3.99

These books can be ordered from Amazon and other booksellers.

# LOCAL HISTORY & MEMOIRS FROM APS BOOKS
## (www.andrewsparke.com)

*Aramoana (Andrew Sparke)*
*Bella In The Wych-Elm (Andrew Sparke)*
*Countdown Cath (Cathy Hytner)*
*Croc Curry & Texas Tea: Surviving Nigeria (Paul Dickinson)*
*Glimpses Into Sutton's Past Vol. I & II (Stephen Roberts)*
*Leaving Lewis (Helen Pitt)*
*Magna Carta Wars Of Lincoln Cathedral (Andrew Sparke)*
*More Swings Than Roundabouts (John Wright)*
*Piggery Jokery In Tonga (Andrew Sparke)*
*Rear Gunner (Andrew Sparke)*
*Stutthof (Andrew Sparke)*
*Tales From Pinfold Farm (Helen Pitt)*
*The Devil's Cauldron (Pete Merrill)*
*The Erstwhile Buddhist (Helen Pitt)*
*The Strange Free-Fall Of Fred Ryland (Helen Pitt)*
*The Ways Of Mevagissey (Andrew Sparke)*
*War Shadows (Andrew Sparke)*
*Who Put Bella In The Wych Elm? Vol.1 The Crime Scene Revisited (Alex Merrill)*
*Who Put Bella In The Wych Elm? Vol.2 A Crime Shrouded In Mystery (Alex Merrill)*

Printed in Great Britain
by Amazon